SELF-DETERMINATION
IN THE MIDDLE EAST

SELF-DETERMINATION IN THE MIDDLE EAST

Yosef Gotlieb

PRAEGER

PRAEGER SPECIAL STUDIES • PRAEGER SCIENTIFIC

Library of Congress Cataloging in Publication Data

Gotlieb, Yosef
  Self-determination in the Middle East.

  Bibliography: p.
  Includes index.
  1. Minorities—Near East.   2. Near East—Politics
and government.   3. Near East—Ethnic relations.   I. Title.
JQ1758.A38M53   1982   323.1'56   82-13239
ISBN 0-03-062408-8

Published in 1982 by Praeger Publishers
CBS Educational and Professional Publishing
A division of CBS Inc.
521 Fifth Avenue, New York, New York 10175 U.S.A.

© 1982 Yosef Gotlieb

23456789   052   987654321
Printed in the United States of America

ACKNOWLEDGMENTS

Limits of space prevent me from thanking the many writers and thinkers whose work guided me in the preparation of this book. Among these people are members from the gamut of Middle Eastern nationalities. I hope that this work will serve to honor the quests for freedom in which many of these people are engaged.

I am grateful to the directors of the Curwen Stoddart Memorial Fund, who encouraged my work by making a grant available to me in 1979. The fund was established in memory of Curwen Stoddart, who had dedicated his life to facilitating Arab-Jewish rapprochement. I have earnestly sought to incorporate Professor Stoddart's progressive vision concerning the peaceful coexistence of Mideastern peoples into this work.

I am also indebted to the World Jewish Congress (WJC) and particularly to its executive director, Israel Singer, for enabling me to pursue the research that informs this work during my tenure as director of the WJCs Project for the Study of Middle Eastern Nationalities. During this project I benefited from the research assistance and friendship of Wilhelm ("Bill") Figueroa.

A special thanks is due to Dr. Ismet Sherrif Vanly, whose comments on my chapter dealing with the Kurdish national movement proved most helpful to me.

My greatest appreciation goes to my wife, Donna Eve Nevel, without whose intellectual prowess and analytic abilities this work would not have succeeded.

CONTENTS

SELF-DETERMINATION
IN THE MIDDLE EAST

1

SELF-DETERMINATION IN
THE MIDDLE EAST:
THE ENDURANCE OF TURMOIL

The great expanse of territory extending from the westernmost reaches of northern Africa to lands east of the Tigris and Euphrates rivers, from Asia Minor to the deepest Sudan, encompasses those countries presently under Arab rule, that is, the "Arab world." These stretches of land straddle the African and Asian continents and vary from desert wilderness to snow-covered mountains.

Ethnically, the "Arab world" is a highly heterogeneous region. Multitudes of Kurds populate the Middle East's northern tier along with Arabs, Azerbaijanis, Baluch, Persians, Turcomans, and other Turks. Arabs and Jews, Armenians and Assyrians, Druze and self-described "Phoenecians" inhabit Syria, Iraq, Lebanon, and Jordan. While the Arabian Peninsula is correctly described as a "sea of Arabdom," Dhofaris, Persians, and other ethnic groups have struck roots deep in Islam's heartland.

Across the Red Sea, in Africa, Nubians and other ethnic Africans inhabit Djibouti and the south of the Sudan. Also living in these countries are ethnic Somalis, who make up the majority of the population in Somalia and Eritrea. Just north, in Egypt, live the Copts, a small minority who some Egyptians maintain represent the contemporary manifestation of primordial Egypt. To the west of Egypt, in Libya, Algeria, and Morocco, Berber language and culture form the social basis of the Maghrebian hinterland. Mauritania, as its name denotes, is the "land of the Moors," a hybrid people of mixed Arab-Berber ancestry.

As diverse as the Middle East is ethnically, its linguistic and cultural richness makes the region a mosaic of peoples. Arabic language and culture are dominant in the region, but to depict the Middle East as a vast Arab domain belies the region's manifest heterogeneity.

1

According to the conventional portrayal of the Middle East, the Palestinian problem is the foremost issue frustrating efforts to achieve stability in the region. While the Palestinian problem remains a primary factor in the continuing hostilities embroiling the Middle East, it is inseparable from a pervasive, albeit obscured malaise affecting all the peoples populating the region. As indicated by the considerable ethnic and religious unrest that has wracked the region of late, the suppression of submerged Middle Eastern nationalities by the dominant ruling elites in the area is the major underpinning of the enduring turmoil.

In recent years, outbursts of disaffection have torn through northern Africa. For the first time in decades, riots have broken out in the Maghreb, the result of Berber discontent concerning government plans to further the Arabization of Algerian society. In a war against Morocco, the Polisario continue to press for an independent state. Lately, the Copts have raised their voices in protest regarding a recent referendum that makes Islam the official religion of Egypt. In Egypt and the Sudan, as well as elsewhere in the Arab world, the Ikhwan al-Musselmeen (the Moslem Brotherhood) has resurged, which makes the spread of extremist Islam an increasing danger. In the Horn of Africa, which is a geopolitical tangent of the Middle East, the Eritrean and Ogaden conflicts continue to produce relentless bloodshed.

Confrontations abound elsewhere in the Middle East. Since the 1975-76 civil war, Lebanon has fallen victim to ongoing hostilities between Moslems and Christians. The Syrian army, whose arrival in Lebanon after the civil war was sought and welcomed by many Lebanese, has since remained in virtual occupation of that country. In effect, Lebanon has now been gerrymandered into a disharmonious constellation of distinct entities, each with separate loyalties to various Middle Eastern states. This fragmentation has eroded the foundation of the Lebanese republic. In view of Lebanon's history, it is questionable whether the republic, a byproduct of French imperialism, ever had a basis in anything other than political and commercial expediency.

Syria, despite the relative endurance of President Hafez al-Assad's regime, has recently been plagued by fissures along ethnoreligious lines. President Assad, who is of the minority Alawite sect, seized power ten years ago in a coup d'etat that overthrew a government led by a rival Baathist party faction. While his regime has outlasted all previous governments of postindependence Syria, Assad's rule is increasingly unpopular among the predominantly Sunni Syrian citizenry. Alawites occupy a disproportionate number of leading positions in the Syrian economy, as well as in the political and military elites. These facts have provided convenient pretexts for the terrorist outrages of the Ikhwan al-Musselmeen, who have carried out a number of attacks in Damascus, Allepo, and Latakia. The ranks of those in opposition to the Baathist regime have swelled, imperiling the continuation of President Assad's rule. It is, therefore, quite understandable that the old nostalgia for "Greater Syria," which entails the unification of Lebanon and historic Palestine with Syria, has emerged among the Syrian leaders. A paper merger of Syria with Libya that was recently agreed to is similarly intended as a diversion of attention from President Assad's misrule.

Turkey, long considered the bastion of the West in the world of Asian Islam, is undergoing unprecedented challenges to its policies of "turkification," in addition to the convulsions that the society has suffered as a result of leftist/rightist political fighting. As order appears to have been restored by the military junta now controlling the country, the genocide committed against the Armenians as a result of the Young Turks' Revolution, and the continued and severe restrictions on non-Turkish language and culture are being avenged by Armenian nationalist groups operating in Europe and Turkey. Additionally, the Kurds of Turkey, whose communal existence has been officially denied by the Turkish authorities for decades, have renewed their demands for autonomy through the Apolun and other Kurdish nationalist movements operating clandestinely in eastern Turkey. In fact, the junta has adopted extensive measures in imposing martial control over the Kurdish regions and in remanding large numbers of Kurdish activists.

Turkish Kurdistan is only a small part of a contiguous territory encompassing large areas of Iraq, Iran, and Syria; these areas are populated almost exclusively by Kurds. In Iraq alone, at least 25 percent of the overall population are Kurds living in Kurdistan. These Kurds have remained in Iraq despite the genocidal wars launched against them throughout the past two decades by the various governments that have seized the instruments of state in Iraq.

In neighboring Iran, Kurdistan extends into the province known by that name, as well as into Azerbaijan and Kermanshah provinces. Since the Islamic Revolution, the Kurdish guerrilla forces known as the peshmergas have been waging a continuous campaign to win autonomy. They have posed a serious threat to the Iranian military forces. As Iraq and Iran continued their war, the Kurdish issue became a pawn used increasingly by one regime against the other.

While the Kurds are the strongest and best organized of Iran's national minorities, they are by no means the only insurgent nationality that Tehran must contend with. In a country whose population consists of at least 60 percent non-Persian ethnics, the many millions of Azerbaijanis, Baluch, and Turcomans have also been pressing for greater autonomy. Moreover, the struggle by these nationalities for communal rights has gone beyond Iran's frontiers and has led to terrorist attacks launched in Europe and elsewhere. These attacks reflect growing discontent among the demographically Arab population of Iran's Khuzestan's (Arabestan) province. It is this province that had been occupied by Iraq following their 1980 invasion of Iran. According to Baghdad, the region had been "liberated" for the sake of "Arabism."

These conflicts, as well as similar imbroglios, indicate the significant position of submerged nationalities in the Middle East. In a region conspicuous for its coups d'etat, dictatorships, monarchies, and sheikdoms, there is a direct relationship between these forms of governmental rule and the suppression of ethnonational groups. The motivations behind the governmental policies toward Middle Eastern ethnic groups—along with the proliferation over the past 50 years of states that do not cohere with the underlying historic and demographic realities of the region—are pervasive features of Middle Eastern governments today. Further, the instruments of power in these states are concentrated in the hands of elites who legitimize their governments by mobilizing totalitarian creeds such as pan-Islamism and pan-Arabism. The imposition of these ideologies has disenfranchised important sectors of the region's inhabitants. The region has been conventionally defined in terms of these legitimizing creeds, which, in effect, deny self-determination to millions of non-Moslem or non-Arab people. Furthermore, the authoritarianism accompanying these ideologies denies democratic government for, and civil liberties to, the overwhelming majority of inhabitants of the Middle East, including Moslem Arabs.

The origins of rule in the contemporary Middle East result from three factors: the deottomanization of the region; the British and French colonization of the Middle East; and the transfer of power from the withdrawing colonial regimes to the Young Turks, the Pahlavi dynasts, and most importantly to Arab elites. The signal event in these three factors was the Arab Revolt of 1916, in which the Hashemites emerged, with British support, as the rulers of the Hejaz, Transjordan, Iraq, and briefly of Syria as well. The revolt effectively dismantled the Ottoman Empire, particularly the empire's Arab provinces, and replaced them with states, mandates, and protectorates. The boundaries of these polities were determined largely through negotiations between the metropolitan powers alone. The succession of government in these newly created states has been, almost without exception, through the transfer of power to elites, whose right to govern derived from inheritance, military force, or usurpation.

The Arab Revolt emerged out of the desire on the part of the Arab peoples to emancipate themselves from Ottoman domination. Deturkification, the original raison d'être of the revolt, held the promise of independence for the Arab peoples. The yoke of Ottomanism, however, has been substituted by the Arabization of most of the Middle East. Ottoman suzerainty has been replaced by a system of rule that is no less oppressive and that has apportioned much of West Asia and north Africa to Arab rulers. Most of these rulers have obtained their governments by sheer force. Overall, the legitimization of power in the Middle East does not derive from popular mandate but, rather, from the seizing of power by native military and civilian "strongmen."

The manner in which various states in the Middle East came about has produced a number of anamolous circumstances. The Kurdish nation, for example, is divided by artificial frontiers that place integral parts of Kurdistan under Turkish, Iraqi, Syrian, and Iranian control. Similarly, the Azerbaijanis live on territory that has been split between Iranian and Soviet rule, and the Baluch have been divided between Iran and Afghanistan. The tens of millions of Berbers in the Maghreb emancipated from colonial oppression through the various northern African liberation movements that were active in the 1950s and 1960s, now find themselves oppressed by Arabism in language, culture, and politics. The Berbers are resisting the loss of their traditional identity and the forced adoption of Arab nationalism and culture.

The significance of Arabism to the peoples of the Middle East is an important one. The pan-Arab idea afforded—despite its ad hoc usage of Islamic religious fervor—a secular framework by which the Sunni, Shiite, and Christian Arabs could band together to overthrow Turkish domination and arrest European colonization and superpower exploitation. In this respect, Arabism has played an indispensable role in the achievement of progress in the Middle East. The pan-Arab idea has, however, exceeded its initial purpose and has extended beyond its legitimate aims. It has become a suppressive system preventing the national self-expression of the scores of millions of non-Arabs indigenous to the Middle East. The pan-Arabist system has glossed over deep-seated divisions that must be acknowledged if the various national and religious groups in the Middle East are to achieve a modus vivendi with one another. The force of pan-Arabism has ceased being an emancipatory instrument. Instead, it has become a lever for the perpetuation of power by the ruling elites, and it acts to preserve the hodgepodge "nations" these rulers have inherited.

A residual effect of the maintenance of Middle Eastern states is the global influence of Arabist leaders. The Saudi Arabian monarchy and the Persian Gulf sheiks, for example, have attained an unparalleled role in world affairs owing to their petroleum resources and political clout, both of which they are not eager to relinquish. Similarly, Iraq's oil wealth is concentrated beneath the lands of Iraqi-controlled Kurdistan: any autonomy that might be gained by the Kurds could, therefore, not only threaten the political base of Iraqi leaders but their economic foundations as well. An analogous situation exists in the case of Iran's Khuzestan's province: much of Iran's oil is located beneath that demographically Arab province. Any measure of autonomy received by the Khuzestanis could, therefore, presage the independence of the province and lead to the bankruptcy of the Islamic republic.

The status of all submerged nationalities in the Middle East directly affects the power bases of the presently governing elites. The possible loss of control over important state power bases that ethnic autonomy would induce indubitably underlies the suppression of the submerged nationalities of the Middle East.

The suppression of Middle Eastern "minorities" is an integral part of regional affairs, and this aspect of the contemporary Middle East is central to any analysis of ongoing developments in the region. Further, a cogent perspective on the Middle East can be gained only through an appreciation of the historical processes that have shaped the region over the last hundred years. These processes—the socio-economic, the political, and the strategic—have interacted in a continuous dynamic. It is impossible to comprehend the Middle East in all its fullness without analyzing these individual historical processes, as well as their composite effect. The Middle East has not come to be so fraught with instability and violence by accident or fate: an identifiable series of events, each fulfilling a specific function, have interacted and shaped the Middle East into its current form. The analysis of the processes at work in the Middle East and their historical interaction comprises the material covered below.

The time frame to which this study refers begins with the crumbling of the Ottoman Empire under Sultan Abdul-Hamid, culminating in the destruction of the empire during World War I. Since the lands of the Middle East had been ruled mostly by the Ottomans, the dissolution of the empire led to the creation of a power vacuum in the region. In the postwar period, as a result of the designs made prior to and during the war by the Entente powers, the power vacuum was filled by European control over the Middle East through intensified European economic initiative in the region. The penetration of European capital in the Middle East had commenced in earnest during the second half of the nineteenth century. Over time, European economic activity changed in nature from private enterprise in cooperation with the European governments to imperial state interests concerned with the optimization of economic and strategic issues. The introduction of private U.S. economic endeavor in the region, particularly through the activities of the U.S. multinational petroleum concerns, enhanced the West's interests in the affairs of the region. The final stage in the contemporary history of the Middle East entailed the discontinuation of formal European control over the Middle Eastern countries and their replacement by power centers designated by the Europeans to succeed them. This transfer of overt control, from European colonial to indigenous power centers, accomplished the termination of direct foreign rule. This transfer of control was implemented, however, in a way that largely preserved the economic and strategic interests of the Western powers.

The period under study consists, therefore, of the deottomanization of the region, the introduction of foreign control, and the decolonization of the region in favor of a new political system in which power centers have been transformed into ruling elites who purportedly serve the needs and aspirations of the peoples over which they rule.

The relative ease with which the Ottoman Empire was destroyed and replaced by colonial, and later indigenous, control was a direct result of the inherent decrepitude of the Ottoman regime. The seeds for self-destruction were contained within the very nature of the empire. The empire, therefore, must be understood, especially against the backdrop of the political culture of the Middle East, from its rise until its demise during World War I.

The historical processes that have interacted to produce the present political landscape of states, liberation movements, and other forces in the Middle East were shaped by the functions they fulfilled at the time of their inception. It is important to identify those economic and political interests that have been advanced by shaping the Middle East into its contemporary national boundaries. There is a curious divergence between the historical and contemporary realities of the peoples residing in the region and the mode of government and society presently imposed on them. The current system of government and society represents elites and interests that are far removed from the genuine needs and concerns of the Middle Eastern masses.

The proliferation of Arab states over the past 50 years, the emergence of the oil weapon and the concomitant political clout it engenders, and the realignment of global policies around the question of Palestine function in the interests of two very disparate groups. These groups—the indigenous power centers of the Middle East and the Western concerns and governments that have installed and have kept them in power—have evolved into a relationship for the purpose of mutual gain. States have been created and elites generated to govern them. These elites, in reality, operate more on their own behalf and that of the multinational petroleum companies that prop them than for the benefit of their citizens. That states were created where none previously existed and that kings were crowned and rulers invested where there were no kingdoms is indicative of the misbegotten system that overlays the Middle East.

These contemporary realities are the manifestations of historical processes. The existence of 21 Arab states and the prosecution of

claims for another two Arab states (the Palestine Liberation Organization's Palestinian state and the Saharan Arab Democratic Republic
of the Polisaro) involve the vast territory stretching from Asia west
of Iran and south of Turkey, including all of Africa north of the Sahara.
Linguistically, the people residing in the area speak Arabic, Kurdish,
Turkish, Hebrew, Persian, Armenian, Somali, Berber, and numerous
other tongues in addition to the colonial languages of English, French,
and Italian. A multitude of ethnonational groups reside in the region,
including: Arabs, Azerbaijanis, Turcomans, Persians, Jews, Kurds,
Yazidis, Copts, Armenians, Somalis, Dhofaris, Nubians, Berbers,
and Moors. The religious communities present in the region include
Shiite, Sunni, and other Moslems, Jews, Bahais, Zoroastrians, Copts,
animists, and virtually the entire spectrum of Christian denominations.
What all of this ethnic, linguistic, cultural, racial, and religious diversity indicates is that the conventional portrayal of the Middle East
as a homogeneous sea of Arabdom bounded by Moslem Iran and Turkey
has been projected by the ruling groups of the region in order to preserve elitist power. Reducing the many conflicts affecting the Middle
East into one single Arab-Israel conflict transforms the myriad of
ethnonational confrontations in the region to one set of imbroglios.
This enables the ruling elites to consolidate their power, since they
are obliged to utilize their resources and political power as weapons
in the Arab-Israel conflict. In reality, these weapons are not instruments for defending nations, but rather tools for increasing the economic and political power of self-interested elites.

The mobilization of pan-Arabist and pan-Islamic legitimizing
creeds has facilitated mutual support between the various nonrepresentative regimes in the region and has further obfuscated the demographic realities of the region to the outside world. It has imposed
Arab political, economic, linguistic, and cultural hegemony on all
ethnonational sectors of the heterogeneous Middle East and has completely clouded the class and other underlying issues and conflicts
afflicting the region.

The Palestinian issue, which is presumed to be the crux of the
Arab-Israel conflict, is the only question of self-determination in the
Middle East that has been extensively examined by the international
community. Given the attention the issue has received, it is both iro-
nic and tragic that the Palestinians still suffer their plight while anti-
Zionist and anti-Semitic resolutions are enacted as the primary form
of support for Palestinian national rights. The Arab elites and their
allies have cited Israeli government policies to support bombastic
claims made against Israel and Zionism. The continued occupation of
Arab lands and the insensitivity of certain Israeli policies are repre-
hensible. As injurious as certain Israeli policies are, however, they
have been magnified out of proportion in order to bolster the malicious

charges of racism and imperialism leveled against Israel, and its raison d'être, Zionism. Additionally, while many of the Israeli actions have been deplorable, it must be recalled that they take place against the background of unabating exclusivism and hostility generated against Israel by neighboring Arab elites. Moreover, though Zionism is an ideology seeking to create a particular type of sociopolitical entity in the Middle East, it does not propose to do so in an effort to achieve regional hegemony or in order to subjugate the non-Jewish peoples of the Middle East. Zionism and Israel have been cited as the root cause of most of the turmoil plaguing the Middle East. In reality, however, Zionism is the basis for a constructive movement that seeks to provide the Jewish people with the resources necessary for national well-being. Zionism is the movement for Jewish self-determination. Given the history of the Jewish people, Israel, the instrument of Zionism, has just as much right to exist as does any other state on the face of the globe.

It cannot, however, be denied that the implementation of Zionism did in some way dispossess another group, the Palestinians. Whether this could or could not have been avoided and to what extent the dispossession was actually attained is a subject for future debate. As attested, though, by the numerous proposals for coexistence between an independent Israel and Palestine, Zionism and Palestinianism are not inherently incompatible. There is in Israel today a sector of the population whose religious and nationalistic fervor, if it were unchecked by the large number of moderate and dovish Israelis, would block the prospects for coexistence with the Palestinian people. However, this zealous block, while influential and powerful under the Likud coalition, represents neither the ideology of mainstream Zionism nor the opinions of many within the Israeli public. Israel must, for numerous reasons, cede territories and alter policies, but this does not require nor should it demand the renouncing of its Zionist foundations.

A detailed explanation of the Palestinian problem cannot, of course, be offered in the course of a few paragraphs in the introduction to a book dealing with the root causes of suppression in the Middle East. Certainly, there have been considerable activities undertaken by the Zionist movement and Israel that would serve to reinforce Arab fears concerning Zionism. On the other hand, there are ample Arab hostility and terror committed in the name of Palestinianism to discourage even the most dovish Israeli in the pursuit of coexistence with the Palestinian people. An analysis of the manner in which both Israeli and Palestinian fears and actions have reinforced mutual belligerence will be provided in the concluding chapter of this book. This manipulation of the Palestinian cause by the Arab ruling elites, who have used the continued suffering of the Palestinians as a diversion from their own misdoings, will also be discussed. The Palestinian problem has offered a critically important pretext for the waging of war, economic blockades, and oil "shortages" by the region's ruling elites. These consequences of the Palestinian conflict have enhanced the political and economic interests of the cliques governing the Middle East. This exploitation of the Palestinian cause does not, however, detract from the legitimacy of the Palestinian movement for self-determination.

The preeminent feature of pan-Arabism and pan-Islamism today is support for the Palestinian cause or, to state it more correctly, the elimination of Israel and Zionism in the name of Palestinianism. In the widely propagated rhetoric of the pan-Arabists, Zionism and Palestinianism are intrinsically at cross-purposes. The Arab elites have represented the achievement of Palestinian self-determination as being contingent on the dezionization of Israel. The Palestinian movement, therefore, is formulated as being essentially anti-Zionist, as opposed to pro-Palestinian. The conduct of discourse on this issue in the above terms has led only to frustration and uncompromising policies on Israel's part, which is, of course, a natural reaction of a society whose existence is constantly assailed.

The alleged inherent evils of Zionism have been emphasized so much that objective consideration of its role in Middle Eastern affairs and its meaning to the world Jewish community is no longer possible. This is attributable to the anti-Zionist campaign that the Arab elites have been waging for the past 50 years. Given the ramifications of the anti-Zionist campaign, a critical understanding of the significance of Zionism to the Moslem ruling elites is imperative. This significance is found in the success of one Middle Eastern, non-Arab people, the Jews, to achieve independence. This independence threatens the region's governing elites, since it sets a precedent that is dangerous to the totalitarian system of government now entrenched in the Middle East. The danger of Zionism lies in the possibility that other submerged nationalities in the Middle East may be encouraged to struggle for their own self-determination. This, of course, is an anathema to the authoritarian Middle East elites.

The Middle East conflict, which has been gratuitously and falsely equated with the Arab-Israel conflict, has at its base the right to self-determination for all the peoples of the Middle East. This right applies to Palestinians and other Arabs, as well as to Jews, Kurds, Druze— indeed, to all Middle Eastern ethnonational groups.

The view that the Middle East can be reduced to a simplified model based on overgeneralizations concerning its demography and government contributes significantly to the turmoil in the region. Self-government is a right to which the Palestinians are entitled, but this same right must be granted to the other nationalities in the region. The ascendancy of Arabic language and culture cannot be interpreted as reflecting sociocultural homogeneity. A realignment of the states in the Middle East in tandem with cultural, linguistic, and ethnic diversities inherent to the region is a prerequisite to progress in the area. Accordingly, the redefinition of the Middle East in terms of the region's underlying realities is a necessary antecedent to the achievement of self-determination by the peoples of the region.

2

THE HISTORICAL ANTECEDENTS OF MIDEAST POLITICAL CULTURE

The arrival of the Arab peoples onto the center stage of history followed the birth of Islam. It was Islam, pulsating with the beat of desert life, that propelled the nomadic and sedentary tribes of the Arabian peninsula into Africa and Asia. The evangelical nature of the creed and its weltanschauung as a universal faith served as the fountainhead for a new system of power relations that would forever alter world history.

Islam (lit. "submission to the will of Allah") is a way of being that does not distinguish the "city of God" from the "city of man." It is a creed reflecting divine will and, a fortiori, one that dictates the conduct of human affairs. Founded by the Prophet Mohammed, Islam was born during the seventh century in the Hejaz, now the western part of Saudi Arabia.

Prior to his death in 632 A.D., Mohammed had succeeded in accomplishing feats of herculean proportions. He had transformed the lives of Arabia's inhabitants—the original Arabs—from a pagan-worshiping tribal existence to a society in which monotheism and a divinely sanctioned code of life were central. Moreover, he had forged a novel community based on a particular set of beliefs of his own personal advocacy. The Moslem community, the umma, transcended intertribal hostilities and imposed a new societal order on the people of the desert.

The century following Mohammed's death involved a great expansion for Islam. Conquests resulting in the extension of territories, resources, and rule were undertaken. These conquests assumed the color of a religious imperative as Islam gathered dynamism.

The media for the spread of Islam were Arabic language and script. That Mohammed himself was an Arab and that Islam was generated in Arabia gave the Arabs sweeping out of the desert an air of aristocracy and self-importance that has remained in dar al-Islam (the House of Islam) until the present. Prior to the onset of modern (that is, Western) nationalism over the last century, the relationship between Islam and the Arabs has been difficult to define clearly. Initially, the identity between Moslems and Arabs was inextricable, but as the dar al-Islam became more diverse with respect to language and culture, Arabs became a political elite rather than the sole bearers of Islamic faith. Thereafter, Moslem identity involved adherence to the Five Pillars of Faith, rather than a particular ethnic origin.

At the beginning of Islamic rule, the center of authority in the dar al-Islam was the caliph (the "successor" to Mohammed). The caliphate was an office that, by virtue of the identity between the religious and political realms in Islam, embodied the governance of the affairs of state as well as religious issues pertaining to dar al-Islam. Eventually, the religious and political offices became differentiated from one another through the creation of the political office, known as the sultanate. At various times during subsequent Islamic history, a sultan would assume the role of caliph, which provided him with a religious aura that made his rule beyond reproach.

The struggle for the caliphate represents the major issues that resulted in the schismatizing of Islam into its orthodox (Sunni) and heterodox (Shiite) branches. The recognition of various caliphs, the battles over the caliphate, and the consequential development of the various Islamic sects is of interest here since the divisions have been long and deep within Islam and the Arab world.

The Sunni-Shiite split led to another form of fragmentation within the nascent umma. The Arab world as such was embroiled in internecine fighting that pitted various tribes and clans against one another. Of these, the Ummayads became triumphant. Shortly after Mohammed's death, the Ummayads were able to impose rule over the various Arab tribes and settlements, and they established the first Islamic state, which had its capital at Damascus. In this state, the Sunni Arabs predominated not only over other Arabs, but over Shiites and other communities in the region. They were able to establish themselves as the guardians of Islam, and accordingly they exacted outrageous tributes from their subjects. The taxation of the non-Arabs was particularly excessive.

The rise of the Ummayad dynasty, however, did not eliminate the intertribal fighting among the Arabs that had begun to spread following the dispute between those favoring a geneological succession of the caliph from among Mohammed's descendants and those advocating alternative methods by which to choose the caliph. Consequently, disaffected Arabs constantly rose in revolt against the Ummayads. Additionally, the non-Arab Moslems joined with the Arab dissidents in attacking the Ummayad state. As a result, the Ummayad state was weakened and eventually gave rise to another Moslem empire, the Abbasid, in which individual Arab elites served among the leadership, but which led to the lessening of Arab influence in the affairs of the umma. The Abbasid and other Moslem empires that subsequently gained control of the Middle East (including the Fatamids, the Mamalukes, and the Seljuk) were Islamic, non-Arab dynasties. As a result, there was an evolution of group identity in the region, according to which Arabic language and tradition enjoyed a special status. This special status did not, however, provide the Arabs with a privileged position in the social structures that were created by the various Moslem empires that governed the region.

THE SUBMERGENCE OF ARAB IDENTITY

The new Moslem identity, transcending race and nationality, did not imply that to be a Moslem was necessarily to be an Arab. Indeed, the great majority of the world's Moslems were, and still are, non-Arabs. To be a Moslem did entail a new group identity in which the Arabs were at the apex of Islam, due to the preeminent role of Arabic language as the medium by which the creed had been propagated and the location of Islam's principal shrine cities (Mecca and Medina) in Arab areas. That Mohammed and the original dar al-Islam were Arabs added to the prestige enjoyed by Arab Moslems.

The submergence of a unique Arab identity distinct from Islamic identity preceded the flourishing of Islam as a civilization, which would come to pervade western Asia, northern and eastern Africa and, for a time, the Iberian Peninsula and other parts of southern Europe. The heights attained by Islam during the medieval period and the relative harmony that existed in the disparate parts of the Moslem empires owed much to the humanistic interpretation of Islam that informed the various Islamic governments throughout the Middle Ages. Islam, introspective and dynamic, produced splendors of architecture, art, philosophy, and medical science that the world had not previously enjoyed.

Islamization, not Arabization, introduced a singularity in the East that permitted the peoples living there, so long as they were Moslems, to fully participate on an equal footing in Moslem civilization. Religion, not ethnonational origin, became the touchstone of community and intercommunal stability.

The Turkish Ottoman regime, which became fully entrenched in the thirteenth and fourteenth centuries, profoundly altered society in the Middle East. The concentration of authority in Constantinople brought most of the empire's territorial holdings under a single, centralized rule and entrenched a feudal agricultural system as the region's economic base. Ottoman control was extended deep into Arabia and northern Africa, and consequently it imposed its Turanian character on a vast realm including Arabs, Kurds, Turks, Berbers, and other groups. With the consolidation of Ottoman rule, the Arabs as well as the other Moslem peoples, became equals in their subjugation under the Turks. This status continued and then worsened throughout the "long stagnation," that is, the nearly 500 years of Ottoman suzerainty. It was not until the age of European colonialism, begun by the invasion of Egypt by Napoleon in 1798, that the Arabic-speaking peoples could begin the process of reversing their submergence.

Napoleon's foray into Egypt and his subsequent frustrated march eastward were undertaken in an effort to disrupt British transit and communication to India. The rivalry between the two imperial powers would play a key role in determining the course of Arab nationalism and sovereignty and the future of the Middle East in general. The region served as a critical juncture in European imperial attempts to strengthen their holdings in the East. It was this initial clash between the two superpowers that indirectly introduced the seeds of Arab nationalism into the region.

Much of the Arab nationalist enterprise can be traced to the activities of Mehemed Ali, a remarkable man who, with the collaboration of his son Ibrahim, managed to remove Egypt from Ottoman control de facto. Mehemed Ali was neither an Arab nor a Turk: he was an Albanian Moslem who was part of a military expedition sent by the sultan to oust Bonaparte. Eventually, Ali became the commander of the sultan's forces in Egypt. Following the withdrawal of Napoleon's forces from the region, Ali became the plenipotentiary of the sultan, a status that he interpreted as having considerable powers. Ali took on the position of viceroy, eventually withholding all but nominal allegience to the sultan while consolidating his control as the ruler of the country. Ali set his sights toward eastern horizons—to Arabia—where, at the behest of the sultan, an Arabian religious revivalist movement with threatening overtones was to be excised before it took root.

The Wahhabi movement, named after its founder, Mohamed ibn Abdul-Wahhab of the Nedj, was the first bud in the blossoming of Arab renaissance. The Arab peoples, suppressed in all ways but religion by the Ottoman authorities, were renewed through the Wahhabi puritan movement. Abdul-Wahhab was a fundamentalist who sought to purify Islam from the secular or heterodox introductions that had been inculcated within dar al-Islam. The Ottoman caliph himself was indicted for his lack of vigilance in the protection of the faith.

The Wahhabis might have been left unmolested had their movement been ensconced far away from the sultan's purview. But the

Wahhabis, whose influence can still be felt in the Arabian Peninsula, found an effective instrument in the House of Sa'ud, the dominant tribe of the Nedj at the time. The Saudis, who had become strict adherents of Wahhabism, launched campaigns against the agents of the "heretical" caliphate in Baghdad and Syria. They ransacked the holy city of Shiism, Karbala, and were generally wreaking havoc upon the Ottoman Empire.

Still in the nominal service of the sultan, Mehemed Ali wad dispatched to Arabia in 1811 to retake the holy cities of Mecca and Medina from the fundamentalists. In seven years, the Hejaz was freed from Wahhabi domination. Shortly after this recapture, the leaders of the Wahhabi strongholds in the Nejd were vanquished. The defeat of Wahhabism, however, precipitated the Arab revival. It was the beginning of the end of Arab dormancy under Ottoman bigotry.

In the years following his successes in Arabia, Mehemed Ali, clearly in search of his own empire, conquered the Sudan and the Red Sea area. In order to stay in the good graces of the sultan, Mehemed Ali's rapidly increasing and impressive military forces intervened on the behalf of the Ottomans during the revolts rocking Greece in 1822. In the following decade, Mehemed Ali's forces had routed the regular Turkish military from their control over Syria. In an effort to preserve his nominal suzerainty, the sultan named Ali's son, Ibrahim, to be governor of Syria, preempting the latter's declaring himself the sovereign of the area. Although the sultan retained official rule over all of his empire, Mehemed Ali had taken effective control of all of Arabdom. This particular status began the separation of the Arab world from the rest of the Middle East and assisted in the development of a unitary Arab identity.

Despite Mehemed Ali's military achievements, he was eventually forced to submit to the European powers' demands that he desist from eroding the Ottoman sultan's rule. From the British point of view, the Ottoman Empire was a necessary part of the colonial effort since it served as a buffer between the Middle East and the Romanov (Russian) Empire. From the colonial vantage point, any change in the Middle East's status quo could only serve to upset the European imperial entente. For this reason, the British dispatched a fleet to Syria in order to assist the Syrians in their efforts to oust Ibrahim Pasha. Syria had become victimized by a new set of taxations necessary to support Ibraham Pasha's governmental extravagances, as well as the provision of tribute to the sultanate. Further, forces destined for the sultan's army had to be conscripted; this, however, entailed the drafting of young Arab men for the purpose of fighting wars that had no relevance to the Arab peoples. Ibrahim Pasha's rule was moderate in terms of tolerance and political rights. His efforts to reinvigorate Syrian Arabism was, of course, a goal that his subjects could sympathize with. These efforts mollified his strong-arm methods of preserving order and increasing his coffers.

Greater Syria, until its assumption of mandatory status under the French in 1920, included the Ottoman sanjaq (a small, semiautonomous unit) of Lebanon, the sanjaq of Jerusalem, as well as the vilayet (a large, provincial-type unit) of Syria, which incorporated much of Transjordan. The population of this area included Moslems, Jews, and Christians, Sunnis and Shiites, town dwellers and Bedouins. The Sunni were by far the majority, although the Latakia region was and still is dominated by the Alawite. Transjordan was overwhelmingly Bedouin, and Druze could be found in Lebanon, Syria proper, and Palestine. Transjordan had been terribly underdeveloped under the Ottoman reign and especially during the reign of Ibrahim Pasha, when the country was doubly taxed in service both to the sultan as well as to Mehemed Ali protodynasty.

EUROPEAN IMPERIALISM AND OTTOMAN FEUDALISM

Syria had been so depleted that it could offer no social services to its citizenry. As late as the 1840s, no secondary educational facilities and libraries could be found in the entire pashalik. No medical resources existed; in short, the country's feudal status could hardly be worse. Syria was festering under the decadent system imposed by the Ottomans. The area could offer no indigenous resistance of its own, since its resources were being drained by intersectarian fighting between the Durze and the Maronites. The country was ripe, therefore, for imperial infiltration and machination. The advance guard of what would become European domination of the countries were Christian missionaries who, interestingly enough, carried the germs of Arab nationalism with them.

The Christian, mainly Maronite, communities of Lebanon and the Syrian hinterland had been present there since the initial stirrings of Christianity. Their numbers were reinforced during the eleventh and twelfth centuries with the coming of the crusaders. A number of monasteries and other Christian religious centers had been cloistered in their midst, silently preserving the literary arts and sciences during the Ottoman's decadent ascendancy. The various Catholic orders had undergone discrimination and some persecution during the eighteenth and nineteenth centuries. The relaxation of societal fetters that discriminated against the Christians—an accomplishment of Ibrahim Pasha's rule of relative tolerance—opened the way for Christian evangelicalism. The renewed missionary activities came not only from the Catholics, but perhaps more importantly from Protestants, notably U.S. Presbyterians. Competition ensued between the Catholics, whose

Maronite, Lazarist, and Carmelite communities were relatively well rooted in Lebanon, and the U.S. missionaries. The latter were free from all associations with the Levant, and there was a certain exoticness about them, including the mystique of money, that gave them a receptivity among the native population.

The missionary activities provided the area with its first exposure to modern secondary schools—where the language of instruction was, significantly, Arabic—and to Arabic-type printing presses. Aside from the hand presses that could be found in monasteries for the reproduction of religious tracts, there were no printing presses in Lebanon and few books could be found in the province. The meaning of this poverty was the retardation of literary Arabic, a language that is rich and that served as the repository of the Arab national will during the Ottoman subjugation of Arab culture. Arabic language, the language of Islam, had been the medium for the Arabization of the umma. Its disuse was both a sign and a cause of the disease afflicting the Arab peoples. The renaissance of the Arabic language was, therefore, a necessary condition for the Arab revival.

The creation of an educational system, while implemented by the missionaries for religious purposes, sparked the beginning of a specifically Arab self-identity among the first generations of educated Syrians. Mehemed Ali had imposed Arab identity as part of his attempts to create his own empire. The new Arab national movement, though, was a spontaneous product of authentic Arab revulsion of Ottoman domination.

THE ARAB REVIVAL

Two of the newly educated Syrians stand out particularly as initiators of the Arab revival. Nasif Yazeji and Butrus Bustani were both Lebanese Christians. Yazeji became the leading Arabic philologist and a creator of grammars, dictionaries, and other books necessary to recharge the Arabic language. A reading of his achievements reminds one of the activities of Eliezer Ben-Yehudah, a Zionist leader who was largely responsible for the revitalization of Hebrew. It is mainly through Yazeji's actions that the Arabic language emerged from its long dormancy.

Bustani endeavored to revitalize Arabic by way of an encyclopedic examination of classical Arabic literature. He founded the first Arab-language journal in Syria, Nafir Suriya, in which he called for harmony between the various communities of Syria as well as for the education of the Syrian people in order to promote patriotism. Bustani agitated for good civic behavior, self-respect, and dignity. His proto-Arabism did not, however, specify the nature of the community to

which the readers of Nafir Suriya were to pledge their allegience.
Was it to Phoenecian nationalism, Arab solidarity, universalism,
Syrian nationalism, or a combination of any of these that was to command the loyalty of the nascent Arab movement? The answer to this
question remained elusive and vexing.

Bustani and Yazeji were among the founders of an Arab Christian
association founded under the tutelage of the missionaries. This association, the Society of Arts and Sciences, was to be scholarly in nature.
However, it could not avoid the issues and ambiguity of cultural and
national identity.

Succeeding the Society of Arts and Sciences were similar organizations called the Oriental Society and the Syrian Scientific Society.
The latter gave a much more specific definition of the community to
which its members belonged. It was an organization composed of both
Christians and Moslems—thus being the first intercommunal effort of
its kind—providing some transcendent, that is, Syrian, identity to the
admixture of ethnicities to which the intellectuals belonged. A distinc-
tively Arab flavor was given to the society after the writing and propagation of a poem by Ibrahim Yazeji, Nasif Yazeji's son. The poem
exhorted the subjugated Arab peoples to recall their freedom and past
glories, to note their present conditions under the despised Ottomans,
and to seek a renaissance of their heritage. It is from this poem that
the famous rallying cry of Arab nationalism "Arise ye Arabs, and
Awake!" derives.

In an effort to placate the Europeans, whose anger had been
aroused by the Ottoman mistreatment of Christians, the sultan set
forward reforms introduced by decrees known as the Hatti Sherrif
(1839) and the Hatti Humayun (1856). The decadence of Ottoman feudalism had, however, attained such an abysmal state that an internecine struggle ensued between the peasantry and the clergy on the one
hand and the landed classes on the other. In 1857 this struggle was
characterized by interclass conflict within the Maronite community.
In the Druze-dominated south, where large numbers of Christians had
migrated over the course of the previous century in order to escape
persecution from Sunni Moslems, the Maronite peasantry launched an
uprising against the Druze landowners. This event fueled the fire between the various communities, and in 1860 a Druze pogrom against
the Christians transpired, forcing the latter to retreat to the cities
north and east, including Damascus. In Damascus, 11,000 Christians
were said to have been massacred when a Moslem mob attacked the
Christian quarter of the city in 1860.

The sectarian violence afforded the European powers the opportunity they had sought to fulfill their "responsibilities" in the region.
The Maronites had been favored by the French; the Druze, in turn,
had been courted by the British. The Ottomans viewed the sectarian

strife as an opportunity to reassert their domination over the areas that had been weakened by Ibrahim Pasha's policies of double taxation.

The Europeans and Ottomans reached an accord concerning the administration of Syria in 1864. The accord, the Reglement Organique, stipulated that Syria would be divided into two provinces and a sanjaq. The provinces were to be governed by a governor general who would be directly responsible to the sultan. Lebanon, which was then a semi-autonomous sanjaq, was to be administered locally according to the status quo of the time, that is, along feudal sectarian lines. The feudal leaders would constitute a representative council that would advise the sultan's governors on policy. The government of Lebanon was, in fact, merely an alignment of sects with a particular socioeconomic hierarchy. This form of government has persisted in modified form until the present.

The perfidy and exploitation engendered by the feudal system and its concomitant intersectarian hostility became the catalyst by which the young, predominantly Christian and Druze intellectuals arrived at a communal identity transcending the loathsome ethnonational and economic roles to which the imperialists had relegated them. In this effort to arrive at a transcendent identity, two essential themes have since remained integral to the Arab national movement: liberty for the Arab peoples from foreign domination and the alteration of the socioeconomic system that lends itself to such domination. Therefore, the struggle for independence (although the definition of the community to be granted independence was still unresolved) and the introduction of a patronage or socialist economic system became the touchstones for the movements for Arab independence (Arab nationalism) and the movements for Arab supremacy (Arabism or pan-Arabism).

The corruption of the Ottoman system, the arrogance and cruelty of its officials, and its inherent quality of extracting indigenous material and human resources for imperial use by the sultanate were the sine qua non of the Middle East in the last quarter of the nineteenth century. The terrible excesses of Sultan Abdul-Hamid's regime, which followed the incompetence and corruption of Abdul-Aziz's suzerainty, provided the necessary pretext for the dismantlement of the empire.

Although the French and British had colluded with the Ottomans with respect to the administration of Greater Syria, the two powers were not beyond compelling the "sick man of Europe" into implementing actions conducive to the regional interests of the European powers. The sultanate was in no position to resist these demands, considering the threat posed by the Romanov Empire in Russia. Ottoman stagnation and debauchery under Abdul-Hamid contributed not only to the Arab national movement, but to the Armenian, Kurdish, Azeri, and other movements as well. While the 1876 constitution (which was never implemented) provided for the equality of the various peoples living under the Turkish regime, the status of the Arab peoples was not altered.

The administrative units into which Syria had been divided during the reign of Abdul-Aziz were further fragmented under the rule
of Abdul-Hamid. Syria was divided into the vilayets of Beirut, Syria,
and Allepo and into the sanjaqs of Lebanon and Jerusalem. To the east
of Syria, Mesopotamia had been divided into the vilayets of Basra,
Mosul, and Baghdad. The sultan's attempts to exercise absolute political authority over the Arabian Peninsula and his claim to the caliphate
were frustrated by the sherrif of Mecca and Medina. The Houses of
Ibn Saud of the Nedj and Ibn Rashid of Shammar in northeastern Arabia
were also protective of their sovereignty, although the latter would
prove particularly loyal to the Ottoman Empire during the 1916 Arab
Revolt. The holdings in Africa—Egypt, the Sudan, Tunisia, Algeria,
Cyrenica, and Tripolitania—were lost one at a time to the European
powers: Egypt to England, Tunisia and Algeria to the French, and the
two constituent parts of Libya to Italy.

The political fortunes of the Ottoman Empire were rapidly slip-
ping as the Romanovs pressed their strategic interests forward during
the latter part of the nineteenth century. Not to be outdone, the French
and British as well as the Italians also asserted demands on territorial
objects of the Ottoman Empire. Drastic action was necessary in order
to preserve the Sublime Porte. Sultan Abdul-Hamid thought that it was
essential to reinforce the divine sanction that his title as caliph afforded him. As nominal head of Islam—a title that no one had yet contested
during his reign—the caliph needed to exploit Islam to reinforce his
political authority. It was also imperative that he seek an alliance
with a European power that could offset the British, French, and Italians. The Germans became the patron of the Ottomans. What is important from the point of view of the Arab peoples is the inflated religious role that the sultan assumed with the encouragement of the
Germans.

The Hamadian system of currying favor with the Arabs involved
the intensification of support for Arab-dominated religious institutions,
particularly in Mecca, Medina, and Jerusalem. Abdul-Hamid initiated
a network of intertribal conflicts as a pretext for the reassertion of
military rule. He executed prominent Arab notables and chieftains
who potentially threatened his rule. Additionally, the sultan banished
some particularly troublesome, yet popular, personages to internal
exile under his personal watch in Constantinople. This policy eventually backfired: the remanding of Sherrif Hussein Ibn Ali, of the House
of Bani Hashem (the Hashemites), to Constantinople during the years
1893 to 1908 would provide the Arab Revolt of 1916 with the leadership
it had awaited for so long.

The Hashemites had traditionally retained control of the Holy
Places in the Hejaz. They held sherrifian status; that is, their lineage
derived from the Prophet's family. Ethnically, they were indisputably

Arab, and their claim as descendents of the Prophet and Keeper of
His Holy Places provided them with an aura that could be rivaled by
few other Arab families. Their detention in Constantinople, despite
its material comforts, was an affront to Islam requiring great amends
if the charge of impiety leveled against the caliph was to be avoided.
The sultan/caliph professed Islamic devotion and began to associate
himself with the originator of modern pan-Islamism, Sayid Jamaluddin
al-Afghani. Al-Afghani attempted to adapt Islam to modernity, preach-
ing a doctrine whereby progress and achievement were to be achieved
through the solidarity and independence of all Moslem peoples. The
sultan's charade as a pious caliph did not convince his subjects, and
it was therefore with little difficulty that Abdul-Hamid fell from grace
during the Young Turks' Revolution.

THE DEATH THROES OF OTTOMANISM

The contempt with which the sultanate treated Arabian language
and culture finally succeeded in offending those for whom Arab heritage
had received renewed importance, that is, the budding Arab intelligentsia. The suppression of Arabic language and culture and the in-
sensitive conscription of Syrian Arabs who were to be sent to fight the
Arabs of Yemen (the Yemenites had refused to succumb to the sultan's
rule) were two of the major factors generating the creation of a secret
Arab society by graduates of Beirut's Syrian Protestant College. The
society, which functioned in the 1870s, agitated for the independence
of Syria and Lebanon and for the revitalization of the Arabic language.
The society, at first Christian in composition, advocated armed struggle as a means for terminating the Ottoman domination of the country.
The society, the existence of which ended with an increase in Arab
suppression practiced by Abdul-Hamid, included as one of its original
members Ibrahim Yazeji, a son of the regenator of modern Arabic.
The activities of this secret society were followed by the widespread distribution in Egypt and Syria of the writings of Abdul-Rahman
Kawakebi, a man deeply engrossed in Koranic thought. While al-
Afghani was a pan-Islamist who believed in the renewal of Islam with
all the peoples of the dar al-Islam regarded as equals, Kawakebi believed in a resurgence of Islam that would be dominated by the Arabs
as an elite. He justified this Arab elitism by citing the preeminent
role played by the Arabs in the creation of Islam. Kawakebi's writings
roughly coincided with the occupation of Egypt by the British and the
publication in Paris of the journal l'Independance Arabe, by the Christian Arab nationalist Najib Azuri. Arab nationalism in Azuri's case
meant a commitment to the independence of Syria and Iraq from Ottoman domination. All told, seeds, which would sprout into the Arab

movement as we know it today, were then being sown among the Arab intelligentsia.

Following the advent to power of the Committee of Union and Progress (the CUP, that is, the Young Turks' Revolution), a brief harmony existed between Arab and Turkish nationalists. The constitution that the CUP had imposed on Abdul-Hamid in 1908 granted equality to all nationalities and tongues under the sultanate. The Arabs, as did the Armenians and Kurds, looked forward to a new status under the reconstituted sultanate. An Ottoman-Arab Fraternity (al-Ikha al-Arabi al-Uthmani) was founded in Constantinople in 1908, the purpose of which was the promotion of Arab interests under the constitutional monarchy. The CUP also forced the recognition of the Sherrif Hussein Ibn Ali as the Grand Sherrif and Amir of Mecca by, for example, acknowledging Hussein's legitimacy as Keeper of the Holy Places and rival to the Sultan/Caliph's role as the ascendant of Islam. The famous excesses that would later characterize CUP government also led to the termination of cooperation between the Turkish and Arab nationalists. The CUP suppressed the al-Ikha al-Arabi al-Uthmani, forcing the entire Arab movement to adopt a clandestine character.

The Arab nationalist movement began to assume a "respectable" nature by way of the al-Mutanada al-Adabi (The Literary Club) of Constantinople and the Ottoman Decentralization Party. Both of these above ground organizations served as a watershed for the Arab nationalists of Iraq and Syria, as well as for their leaders in Egypt. Another group, a secret organization devoted to the creation of a dual Turkish-Arab monarchy along the lines of the Austro-Hungarian Empire, was formed in 1909 under the name al-Qathaniya. The membership of this organization included Arab officers in the Turkish forces whose non-Ottoman allegiances were secretly practiced. These officers would later have a key role in the leadership of the nascent Arab national movement.

A second underground organization, Jamiyat al-Arabiya al-Fatat (The Young Arab Society) came together in 1911 at the initiative of seven Moslem Arabs. Al-Fatat sought Arab emancipation from all foreign yokes. The organization prosecuted its goals in an entirely anonymous manner and had a profound influence on the future direction of the national movement. The national movement itself gained the semblance of a unified entity when an Arab congress was convened in Paris in 1912. The congress coincided with the appearance of the Committee of Reform, which like the Party of Decentralization sought greater autonomy from the sultanate. The leaders of the Committee of Reform were prominent individuals who were well-known throughout Greater Syria and Iraq. The goal of decentralization ran counter to the CUP's doctrine of centralized government. The reformists were suppressed, which aroused the anger of the Arab populace throughout Greater Syria and Iraq.

Another Arab congress of 24 delegates, both Moslems and Christians from Syria, was held in Paris from July 18-24, 1913. The proceedings concerned various proposals for insuring the equal participation of Arab citizens in the government of the empire. The Turkish Committee of Union and Progress viewed the Arab parley with such trepidation that they dispatched the party's secretary general in order to arrive at an understanding with the Arab representatives. Remarkably, considering the lack of violence and of Arab nationalist activity generally, the Arabs were able to win their demands for the unrestricted use of Arabic as an official language of state, and reforms were made in the military concerning areas where the Arabs could be forced to serve. Stipulations that three cabinet ministers be Arabs, and that a number of governor generals be Arabs were also agreed to by the Ottoman representative and the Arabs. The negotiated agreement, however, turned out to be a sham settlement: the Young Turks had pursued a policy of placation instead of vigorously attempting to effect reform.

The arrest in early 1914 of Major Aziz Ali al-Mari, an Arab who had served the sultan with great distinction, played a crucial role in mobilizing the Arabs against the Turks. A founder of the al-Qathaniya (this organization was abandoned by its members when a betrayer was found among them), Aziz Ali founded a second organization, al-Ahd ("The Covenant"). The aims of the latter were to be those of al-Qathaniya, but its membership was to be composed solely of Arab militarymen in the service of the sultan. Like al-Fatat, al-Ahd was kept secret until the two groups amalgamated in 1915. Charged with corruption and treason, al-Mari's trial and his condemnation to death became a causa belle within the Arab world, which served as a beacon for the Arab national movement. Aziz Ali's release was secured after the intervention of the European powers, particularly that of the British. The Arab world, however, used his name as a battle cry in their efforts to rid themselves of Ottoman hegemony. Just as the Dreyfus Affair would rouse the Jews of central Europe to recognize the conditions of discrimination then confronting them and thus fortify Zionism among them, the case of Major al-Mari spotlighted the need of the Arab people to stir from their acceptance of the prevalent status quo.

THE ARAB REVOLT AND THE DEMISE OF THE OTTOMANS

The event that would serve to ignite the Arab world, the Arab Revolt, began, ironically enough, when Abdullah, the son of the Keeper of the Holy Places, Sherrif Hussein, contacted the British agent in Egypt with respect to possible collusion between the infidel imperial power and the sherrifate. Abdullah had been appointed a senator in the Ottoman Parliament. Cognizant of the Ottoman efforts to remove Sherrif Hussein from office and noting the decline of the Ottoman Empire, Abdullah resigned his seat in order to retain his independence. The Hashemites were becoming an almost arrogantly independent power in Arabia, one to which the Ottomans had to defer in matters pertaining to the peninsula. The collaboration between an Arab power center and the British was a fateful alliance that would shape the history of modern Arab history.

The romance between the Germans and the Turks had given an air of urgency to the British interest in the Middle East. Clearly the Ottomans could no longer be relied on, not only because they had been bought by the German imperial endeavor, but also because of the foundering and unpredictability of the failing Ottoman Empire. Mehemed Ali's attempts to attain his own empire by wresting the Arab portions of the Ottoman state from the Sublime Porte proved that a unique Arab identity could be forged. The activities of the various Arab national movements and the great enmity aroused by Ottoman treachery had proven that the Arabs could work integrally for a singular purpose. The British began to court the Arabs, eventually as full allies in their attempts to wreck the cancerous Ottoman Empire. The Hashemites, given their prestige and status within the dar al-Islam, proved to be the best link in the British imperial chain. With the onset of World War I, and the alliance between Turkey and Germany, British aims in the Middle East became even more desperate. Instruments of war were needed, even if the instruments had to be invented.

The sherrif of Mecca, benefiting from the contacts with the British developed by his son Abdullah, was the recipient of rare incentives from the sultan to join him in anti-Allied activities. The sultan was attempting to curry favor from the man he had detained for 15 years, and so the rewards he offered to the sherrif were considerable.

On the other hand, there were indications that Hussein, for so long frustrated in his efforts to win sovereignty over Arabia, might inherit some form of independent rule should the British succeed in their war effort. The exploratory talks evolved into serious negotiations and an exchange of documents between the British and the Hashemites. Throughout the period, the sherrif resisted a call to participate in a jihad, a holy war, that the caliph had proclaimed in an effort to engage religious loyalties as a tool to force the dar al-Islam to support his war effort. That the Keeper of the Holy Places would ignore a call from the pinnacle of Islam was an act without contemporary precedence. It demonstrated above all else that Hussein had reached a critical point in his negotiations with the British in response to Ottoman decadence.

Hussein had not betrayed his negotiations with the British, and at no point did the British expose his discussions with them. Simultaneous negotiations were carried out by Hussein with the Ibn Rashids, the Ibn Sauds, and Imam Yahya of Yemen to ascertain their readiness to desert the Turks and join the British in the achievement of some new power constellation for the Arabian Peninsula. The Ibn Rashids and the Ibn Sauds were embroiled in a blood feud, and the former would later seek the aid of the Turks in their attempts to defeat the latter. The Ibn Sauds, the Keepers of Wahhabism, proved the eventual victors owing to the fact that they supported the victorious side in World War I. Lesser chieftains, such as Sheik Mubarak ibn Sabah of Kuwait (whose descendents still rule that country) retained control of their domain, again due to their fortunate choice of sides in the world war.

The Ottoman caliph's call for jihad found receptive ears throughout Greater Syria. A procession announcing its launching was formed, at which the sherrif, still in 1915, refused to appear. The fever pitch of the jihad threatened to engulf the sherrif as an antihero. Silently, however, the sherrif had been approached by the al-Fatat on behalf of itself, the al-Ahd and other nationalist groups that were preparing for the struggle for independence. They requested that the sherrif join the movement as its leader. At the same time, novel sultanates had been established in Morocco and Egypt; the race for power was on, and Hussein was not one to be left behind. On the other hand, a temperate man by nature, Hussein took his time before ending his relations with the Ottomans. Further, there was some split in the Arab nationalist ranks. Al-Mari, who had gained a special place in the Arab national movement due to his tribulations and those of many of his followers, was inclined to forego the Turks in favor of an alliance with the Europeans. Al-Mari correctly feared, as history would show, that exploitation and advantage would be the price paid by the Arab national movement for European aid.

The negotiations between the British and the Hashemites took a new and serious turn with the exchange of letters between Hussein and Sir Henry McMahon, the British high commissioner for Egypt and the Sudan. The exchange, known as the McMahon Correspondence, would constantly be used since its issuance as the chief legitimizing documents for Arab control over Palestine. The negotiations had proceeded smoothly, except with respect to the administration of Syria. The British had entered into an understanding with the French, which subsequently became known as the Sykes-Picot Agreement. According to the agreement, French possession of parts of Syria would be guaranteed in return for British control of Palestine and Transjordan. What was really happening was that the British were balancing, through their various agents, their responsibilities to their co-colonial power France, their commitments to Sherrif Hussein, and their negotiations with the Zionists, which would eventually lead to the issuance of the Balfour Declaration. All three sets of agreements overlapped in a contradictory fashion with respect to Palestine. The treachery of imperialism would continue unresolved until the present time.

History has demonstrated that all three sets of commitments would interplay to mold the Middle East as we know it today. Sherrif Hussein did eventually reach an understanding with the British, setting off a dynamic process that has resulted in the proliferation of states, constant upheavals, and the instability that has come to characterize that region of the world.

3

THE EMERGENCE OF
MIDEAST ELITIST GOVERNMENT

The emergence of 21 Arab states over the last 50 years has led to a formidable concentration of political and economic power in the hands of Arab rulers. The leaders of the Arab world have effectively promoted their interests and have assumed a pivotal role in global economy and international affairs.

There is, however, an iconoclastic quality to contemporary Arab governments. It is taken for granted that present-day Arab regimes represent the interests of the peoples they govern, and that the Arab ruling elites exercise sovereignty over time-honored boundaries and age-old nations. Gratuitously, it is believed that today's Arab states are the modern manifestations of ancient polities representing homogeneous populations. In reality, the proliferation of Arab states over the past half century has little to do with the needs and aspirations of the Arab masses. The present constellation of power relations in the region is as much a product of foreign interests and external manipulation than of indigenous trends and developments.

The emergence of contemporary Arab governments is a product of the deottomanization and European imperial penetration that has taken place in the Middle East. The needs met by the creation of 21 Arab states were, at least in the earlier part of this century, those of European imperial interests. With the removal of a direct European presence in the Middle East, a power vacuum was created. A transfer of power was effected, which brought to government native power centers whose interests were in tandem with those of the departing imperial authorities. Even in those states where there has been a change in government, this has been carried out without the consent of the governed. Contemporary Arab governments, therefore, serve the interests of Arab elites rather than the nations over which they rule.

In order to understand the roots of contemporary Arab government, it is necessary to take the decrepitude and decay of the Ottoman
Empire fully into account. It is in the demise of the empire that contemporary Arab governments have their beginnings.

THE OTTOMAN EMPIRE

The process leading to the current configuration of power centers and ruling elites in the Middle East has as its departure point the
year 1798, when French armies under Napoleon invaded Egypt and also
attempted to occupy Palestine and Lebanon. Although they were repulsed by forces nominally loyal to the Ottoman sultan, the arrival of
the French in the Middle East arena left a permanent imprint on Egypt
and the rest of the region, transforming that area of the globe economically, politically, and culturally.

The Ottoman Empire emerged on the ruins of an earlier Turkish
empire, the Seljuk, as the result of a successful conquest by Osmanli
Turks, who descended from the Asian steppes in the early sixteenth
century. Within decades, virtually all of Asia west of Persia and most
of northern Africa and the Maghreb were under Ottoman suzerainty.
The boundaries of the new empire extended over much of the dar al-
Islam, and accordingly, the Ottoman sultan claimed the office of caliph, the successorship to the Prophet Mohammed as the chief of Islam. The Ottoman sultans, therefore, wielded considerable power as
both the temporal and spiritual leaders of a vast domain populated by
a variety of indigenous peoples.

Administratively, the empire was divided into vilayets and sanjaqs. Present-day Iraq, for example, consists of three disparate
vilayets, namely those of Mosul, Baghdad, and Basra. Lebanon, while
officially part of Greater Syria, was considered semiautonomous, at
least during the latter part of Ottoman rule and was regarded as the
separate sanjaq of Lebanon. A similar status existed for most of Palestine, much of which was constituted as part of the sanjaq of Jerusalem. The governors of the vilayets and sanjaqs, the valis and beys,
were appointed by the sultan and ruled their lands, at least officially,
in the interests of the Sublime Porte at Constantinople. The real authority exercised by the sultan through his agents, the valis and beys,
diminished the greater the distance was from the Porte. Yemen, for
example, though pledging its loyalty to the Ottomans, was virtually
independent from the empire beyond the payment of tribute to the sultanate.

The status of minorities under the Ottomans was fixed by the
millet system, under which the various non-Moslem communities—
Jews, Chaldeans, Copts, Assyrians, Armenians, and others—were

permitted to conduct their communal affairs according to their respective traditions with little interference from the authorities. The minorities were recognized solely as a group, and their relations with the Ottomans were exercised through a representative council that maintained official status with the sultanate. Taxation, judicial affairs, and educational, cultural, and other communal concerns were regulated and satisfied in compliance with the communities' traditions. In return for their autonomy, the minorities agreed to recognize the paramountcy of the sultan and to acquiesce to his policies. The sultanate also promised to protect the minorities, but discrimination against the Christians and Jews was fairly common throughout the Ottoman realm.

Culturally, the lingua franca of the empire was Turkish, although only a minority of its subjects were Turks. Among the Moslems, the Turks imposed their culture as the dominant one of the empire. The supremacy of one cultural/linguistic matrix over all others has always been the sine qua non of the empires that have dominated the Middle East since the rise of Islam. The Arabs, Kurds, and other Moslems of the realms were subject to particularly stringent cultural subjugation under the Ottomans in addition to their political subordination. As the strength of the empire began to wane, cultural oppression increased. The humiliation and suppression of the Arabic tongue would spark the flames that eventually engulfed the realm.

Economically, the Ottoman's rule led to the abysmal underdevelopment of the region. The empire was locked into a most primitive sort of feudalism, which was conspicuous by the arrest of all technological and industrial innovations. Agriculture grew increasingly inefficient, especially since valuable acreage was squandered on cash cropping, which was necessary for payment of tribute to the Porte. Further, the taxation demanded was in fact double taxation: tribute had to be paid to the empire through the valis and beys; however these subofficialdoms demanded payment in addition to that received for the sultan's coffers. The consequence was, accordingly, the accelerated depletion of indigenous resources.

It is, therefore, no mystery that the European imperialists had a relatively easy time in gaining influence and later control over the region. By the 1880s, the empire was weak and ripe for foreign penetration. Though it took an entire century for the Ottoman Empire to finally totter and fall, the stage was set for its demise by the time Napoleon invaded Egypt.

THE IMPERIAL ENTRENCHMENT

The arrest of French colonization of Egypt at the turn of the nineteenth century, did not, however, impede the spread of European trade and culture in the Middle East. Egypt was one center for the introduction of European civilization into the region, and Syria, specifically Lebanon, was another. The existence of Christian Arab communities, particularly the Maronites and Armenians, provided an important entreé for the Europeans, especially for the French, into the area. Much of the advancement made in Arab literacy—which would subsequently pave the way for the Arab independence movement—would come from the Western missionaries who serviced these Mediterranean Christian communities.

Egypt, that corner of Africa that faces both Europe and Asia, had always played an important role in trade and communications between the continents. It was therefore logical that the French under Napoleon should attempt to occupy the country. The traditional rivalry between the French and the British, heightened by the latter's efforts to secure permanent and fixed supply and communications routes to India and the colonies in the East, resulted in the increased European presence in Egypt and Lebanon. Relations with the government of Egypt were complicated, especially since there were two power centers involved in the country. The first of these involved the local ruler, Mehemed Ali who, ostensibly in the name of the Ottoman sultan, controlled the country and developed it to an extent without precedent in the Ottoman Empire. Mehemed Ali's rule, however, was considerably independent of the Sublime Porte. Egypt, under Ali, was virtually outside of the empire entirely. The French sought influence with Mehemed Ali, and the British, who at the time maintained a strong presence in Constantinople, curried favor with the sultan over Egypt.

The French connection, however, proved stronger, at least in the short run. The French continued to bolster their influence in Egypt, and by 1854 they had obtained a concession from the new viceroy, Mohammed Said Pasha, to construct a canal that would connect the Mediterranean and Red Seas. This link between the Atlantic and Indian Oceans would enormously economize transcontinental shipping between the European metropolises and their eastern colonies. However, given the polarization of influence between Cairo and Constantinople, the British were able to prevent the French Compagnie Universelle du Canal Maritime de Suez from actually beginning construction on the canal until 1858 so that completion was delayed until 1869. This delay was born of the rivalry between the European powers and specifically of the desire by Britain to insure the best possible position for its interests in the construction of the canal. The legal status of the canal was defined to a large extent by the company created to build it. The company was constituted as an Egyptian enterprise, which was subject, however, to French corporate law. It was a public corporation with the majority of shares being split between French shareholders and Egyptian officials. As an Egyptian corporation, the company was required by law to employ Egyptians in 80 percent of its job openings. In real terms, this translated to the establishment of a forced labor situation. Though mollified in later agreements between the Egyptian government and the company, large numbers of Egyptians were conscripted into the canal labor force and subjected to French supervision, since the Egyptian government was forced by the terms of the agreement to supply labor to the company.

The British, with time, began to realize the strategic significance of the canal and commenced efforts to secure a greater degree of control over its functioning. A coup toward this aim was accomplished with the acquisition by Prime Minister Disraeli of 172,602 shares in the company that had been owned by the Egyptian Ottoman viceroy, Khedive Ismail. Though the cost to the British for this acquisition was 100 million francs, this provided them with a considerable bloc of shares in the Suez Canal Company.

With the nationalist's revolt led by Arabi Pasha against the Ottoman regime in 1882, the British entered and occupied Egypt, in order, they claimed, to protect their substantial—though not controlling—interests in the canal company. While the canal remained, at least officially, under Ottoman sovereignty, the British occupation of Egypt placed it under its de facto control. This fact would bear important consequences during World War I.

The Anglo-French influence over the canal, and the subsequent control over Egypt exercised by the British led to European economic hegemony in the Middle East, even under Ottoman political sovereignty. The inconsistency between economic and political control in the Middle East became so significant that, one could argue, World War I was waged in part in order to rectify the incongruity. The untenable inconsistency between mounting European economic power and the Ottoman sovereignty was complicated by German, Russian, and Italian interests in the region. Of these, the Italian was the least significant, since they presented a claim only to the forgotten north African territories of Tripolitania and Cyrenica. The Russians, under the Romanovs, laid claim to the strategic waterways leading into and out of the Sea of Marmara (the Bosphoros and the Dardenelles), as well as parts of northern Turkey. Additionally, Russia claimed rights to greater interventions in the Ottoman Empire due to its self-perceived role as protector of the Christian minorities, specifically, of the Armenians.

Germany, until its defeat in World War I, became an important component of the power relations that defined the Middle East until the onset of the 1916 Arab Revolt. Germany's objective in becoming involved in Middle Eastern affairs had nothing of the tactical character first exhibited by the French and British in their intrusion into the region. While the French and British would eventually learn to view the Middle East as far more than just a link in the chain leading from

Europe to the colonies of the East, the Germans appreciated the Middle East for its material promise. Another difference was Germany's lack of interest in maritime trading and strategic waterways. Concentrating instead on overland objectives that would give it access to subterranean resources, the Germans were the first to appreciate the possible significance of oil in the war effort, as well as future technological innovations. Exemplifying this was the construction by the Germans, in 1902, of the Berlin-Baghdad railroad. The construction of the railroad, particularly with its detour into the mineral-rich Kirkuk district of the Mosul vilayet in Mesopotamia, would define a greatly coveted objective of World War I, namely the search for petroleum deposits.

WORLD WAR I

On the eve of World War I, battle lines had been drawn among the European powers, especially with respect to the Middle East. The Entente powers, including France, Britain, Russia, and Italy, were committed to a strategy that would lead to the dismantlement of the Ottoman Empire. Germany and Turkey opposed this view, with the former country committed to keeping "the sick old man of Europe," Turkey, from collapsing. The ultimate goal for all of the European powers was the same, namely, gaining effective control, either through a puppet regime in Constantinople or through alternative methods, over the lands, peoples, and especially the resources of the Middle East.

At the beginning of the war, Britain stood with the greatest number of outposts in the Middle East. During the nineteenth century, it had succeeded in wresting control over a number of principalities in the southern and western parts of Arabia, including Oman, Yemen, and Kuwait, as well as the sheikdoms on the western side of the Persian Gulf. Additionally, Britain had occupied Egypt, and on the pretext of preserving order in the Sudan, a joint Egyptian-English condominium over Sudan had been established. The French had taken control over Algeria, Tunisia, French Somaliland, French Morocco and had gained hegemony in Greater Syria, particularly in Lebanon. The Italians had Libya, which it had wrested from the Ottomans, and Italian Somaliland. The Russians had succeeded in dividing Iran into northern and southern spheres of influence; they controlled the northern part of the country.

During the war, the Middle East became an important theater of operations, although actual battles in the region took place primarily in the second half of the war. Since the bulk of the fighting during the war took place in and for European possessions, a considerable part of the fighting in the Middle East took place between soldiers native to the region who fought a proxy war for the European powers. Turkey, however, was still constituted as a monarchy, though it was directed by the Western-oriented Committee for Union and Progress (the Young Turks). The Turks were fighting to preserve the Ottoman domains, especially since the war effort was being directed by German military officers in an effort to fortify the German position in the imperial scramble for new possessions. Accompanying the Turkish war effort was the massacre of the Armenians, which, in the infamous year 1915-16 resulted directly or indirectly in the death of an estimated 1.5 million Armenian civilians.

Given that the Entente powers were victorious in the war, it is important to explore the extent of their collaboration with respect to the Middle East during the war years. The French and the British shared a common aim in the dismantlement, allocation, and receipt by the European powers of former Ottoman possessions. Accordingly, at the outset of the war, the Russian claims to the Bosphoros, and Italian "rights" to Libya were agreed to by the Entente powers. In return, Britain and France were freed to prosecute their claims in the region. Discussions between the two Europeans powers produced the Sykes-Picot Agreement, by which the former Ottoman territories of Mesopotamia, Syria, Lebanon, Palestine, and Transjordan were divided between the powers. Given the ascendant role of the French in Greater Syria, both Syria and Lebanon were awarded to the French. British hegemony was recognized in the Hejaz and over most of Iraq and Transjordan. Palestine was defined by an international status. Characterized as "spheres of influence," the Sykes-Picot Agreement in effect served to set the boundaries of areas in which the French and British would be more or less free to pursue their interests. Consequently, with the war's end the imperial status of these territories was formalized. The League of Nations would award these lands to the French and British almost exactly as they had been allocated according to the Sykes-Picot Agreement.

The principles on which the League of Nations was founded demanded that the traditional mode of government practiced by the European imperial powers be changed. The colonial model, by which government of foreign territories was overtly in the hands of the metropolitan powers, was rejected as being inappropriate after the postwar "enlightenment" of the European powers. Nonetheless, European imperialist interests demanded their continued control over the territories. The mode of government adopted would have to satisfy these interests while appearing to safeguard "native" control over the areas involved. The form of administration adopted was the establishment of states over which reliable, indigenous rule could be installed. What this entailed was the awarding of kingships and states to individuals with firm ties to the region and its people. However, only leaders who would act on behalf of European imperial needs, either through necessity or by choice, would be selected.

The perfect candidates for the investure of power in the Middle East were the Hashemites, whose help to the European powers in defeating the Ottomans in the Middle Eastern theater was decisive to the Entente victory. The Hashemites, a clan then led by Hussein ibn Ali, claimed sherrifian status, that is, descendency from the Prophet Mohammed. Hussein ibn Ali was the emir, the guardian, of Islam's most revered sites, Mecca and Medina. This status as the Keeper of the Holy Places, coupled by various trials endured by the Hashemites owing to their power struggle with the Ottoman sultan, made Hussein the ideal leader for the Arab nationalist movement. While the originators of the Arab movement consisted of a small intelligentsia in Beirut, Damascus, and Baghdad, among whom were a number of Arab officers in the Ottoman army, the primary symbol of Arabism with whom the Arab masses could identify remained Hussein. Following a series of clandestine communications between Hussein and his sons and the British officials in Cairo (the McMahon Correspondence), an agreement was reached whereby the British, and to a lesser extent the French, would rely on Arab combatants under Hussein's command in the prosecution of their war aims against the Ottomans. In return, the Hashemites were promised sovereignty over an Arab state that was to encompass large parts of both the French and British spheres of influence.

Under Hussein's command, the desert tribesmen/warriors fought brilliantly and greatly abetted the Entente war aims. This involved an hitherto unprecedented alliance between the Moslem Arabs fighting alongside the Christian Europeans against the chief of Islam, the Ottoman sultan. This was particularly bizarre since the sultan/caliph had declared the war against the Entente powers to be a jihad, which the Arab nationalists under Hussein declined to support. The result as far as the Ottomans were concerned was the destruction of their western holdings. For the Arabs it led to sovereignty over a large expanse of previously Ottoman-held lands, and for the British and French it insured that reliable representatives of their interests would be in control of the lands that were formerly part of the Ottoman Empire.

In the initial McMahon Correspondence, which was arrived at after the Hashemites had secured the backing of the Arab nationalists according to terms stipulated in what had been called the Damascus Protocol, the single Arab state, of which Hussein obviously anticipated becoming king, was to extend throughout the lands controlled by the French and the British. It is important to note that the Damascus Protocol did not call for Arab political control in the Arab lands of northern Africa, over which Arab sovereignty is now exercised.

The vast lands north of the Arabian Peninsula in which the Arabs would claim sovereignty, were too unwieldy to be considered a single unitary state. And so, following the Treaty of Sevres and its successor treaty, that of Lausanne, the British and French received mandates from the League of Nations to govern the newly created states until they attained the maturity necessary for self-government. The polities, which eventually included independent Lebanon and Syria (in the French sphere) and Iraq and Transjordan (in the British sphere), were shaped into states whose boundaries were, significantly, most similar to those stipulated as demarcating the French and British spheres under the Sykes-Picot Agreement. In other words, the creation of states where no cogent "nations" previously existed was a direct byproduct of the imperialist collusion between the European powers. It is significant to note that the original boundaries of the Sykes-Picot Agreement were derived to further as much as possible the strategic and economic interests of the French and the British. Hence, the creation of these states, whose boundaries remain fixed to the present, led to the development of Arab sovereignty in the Middle East for the first time in over a millenium.

The apportioning of rule was carried out in the following way. Hussein became the emir of the Hejaz, that area of the Arabian desert in which Mecca and Medina are located. His son Faisel was originally allocated Syria, sans Lebanon, Jebel Druze, and Latakia. The French were, however, convinced that Faisel was a British agent and they ousted him from Damascus shortly after he proclaimed his kingdom there. Thereafter, Faisel went to Baghdad, where he was proclaimed king of Iraq in the part of Mesopotamia that included the former Ottoman vilayets of Baghdad, Basra, and Mosul. His brother Abdullah claimed Transjordan, of which he was recognized as emir. In this way, four countries were created, despite their lack of a cogent national history, demography, or socioeconomic structure. Further, these states had been awarded to four members of a single family whose policies would subsequently determine the fate of tens of millions of people during the present century.

THE GENESIS OF ARAB POLITICAL RULE

By the 1920s, the independence of the Hejaz (later conquered by the Saudi family of the Nedj and made part of Saudi Arabia), Iraq, Transjordan, Lebanon, Syria, Yemen, and the Persian Gulf sheikdoms was either attained or projected according to a series of mandates or treaties of protection. Repeatedly, the European powers sought men whose standing in the Arab world could serve to legitimize the gerrymandering of the region in which they engaged. Such rulers were elevated to leadership regardless of the wishes of those over which they ruled. They were supported by sizable governmental and personal subsidies provided by the French and British and which were later replaced by the income derived from their oil wealth. This becomes apparent when the history of the various countries are reviewed, and the economic function of their sovereignty vis-à-vis the West is described.

Iraq

From its Hashemite beginnings, Iraq has become one of the chief rivals for the leadership of the Steadfast and Rejectionist Front of Arab States. Iraq has also been beset by a host of sectarian problems, all of which can be viewed against that country's artificial origins. The name "Iraq," which comes, ironically, from the Arabic for "rootedness," is a state composed of the three disparate vilayets of Mosul, Basra, and Baghdad. Historically, these three areas have had very little interaction, and certainly there was no basis for "nationhood" within this country, which is socially divided between Arabs, Kurds, Turcomans, and Persians, and religiously between Sunnis, Shiites and other groups.

The roots of Iraq's statehood can be found in the economic function served by grafting these disparate elements. The economic benefit this grafting served provided the British with the oil-rich regions of Mosul, as well as with overland transport, and transit through the Tigris and Euphrates to the mouth of the Persian Gulf in the Basra vilayet abutting Kuwait. Consequently, the British gained control of the strategic waterways of the Persian Gulf, the Gulf of Oman, and the Straits of Hormuz located between them. In view of the British presence in the Khuzestan province in Iran, which was maintained by British oil concerns operating there with government support, and the protective status of Kuwait and the Persian Gulf sheikdoms under the British, the British government was in effective control of the Persian Gulf area and the outlet to the Indian Ocean. In terms of the economic and strategic interests of the British Empire, the creation of Iraq as it now stands was a most beneficial accomplishment.

The Hashemites governed Iraq until 1958, when a republican-oriented military coup d'etat ended the monarchy. Although the monarchy had gone through three kings in the 26 years since its founding (King Faisel, King Ghazi, and King Faisel II), there had been modifications in the amount of power the crown could exercise. Nonetheless, Iraq had been ruled in the name of the Hashemites until the 1958 coup, despite the fact that its rulers, a Bedouin prince from the desert far from Baghdad and his descendents, ruled over a hodgepodge country that had been artificially created. Since 1958 Iraq has suffered from over 20 coups and countercoups, and that country has yet to have a government whose rule derives from the consent of the governed. The oil revenues accruing to the country has, of course, strengthened the hands of the ruling elite immeasurably.

While the initial benefit of the creation of Iraq to the British has been explained above, it is important to note that throughout the life of the Hashemite crown in Baghdad, the British enjoyed, except for a brief period during World War II, the close alliance of the government of Iraq. Consequently, the British petroleum enterprises functioned expeditiously and profitably under the system whereby British "friendship" with Iraq was guaranteed by treaty. Although a number of anti-British personalities, particularly former Premier Rashid el-Gailani, were involved in shaping Iraqi affairs, the British had, so to speak, the run of the country until the Republican Revolution. Thereafter, British political interests waned, although its economic interests were preserved until 1972, when the Iraqis nationalized the Iraq Oil Company and moved closer into the Soviet orbit.

Jordan

The Hashemite Kingdom of Jordan remains the last bastion of Hashemite rule today. Since its creation in 1921, which Winston Churchill would later boast was accomplished by him "one afternoon in Cairo," and its nominal independence in 1928, Jordan has been ruled by an uninterrupted line of Hashemite rulers. For three decades, King Abdullah governed this former Ottoman "backwater," which had been a desert wasteland populated by nomadic Bedouins before the war. His rule was characterized by extremely close relations with the British, who, in accord with existing realities, controlled everything from foreign affairs to the Jordanian military through a systems of "advisors" attached to the various ministers serving the king. With no infrastructure, cities, or economy, the Hashemite Kingdom under Abdullah existed well into the 1950s on the basis of British subsidy to the royal treasury.

With the death of Abdullah in 1951 and the deposal of his son Talal, Abdullah's grandson, the present-day King Hussein (named after his great-grandfather, the Hashemite patriarch) took over the reigns of government. Though a teenager at the time of his assumption of office, King Hussein embarked on an ambitious development program aimed at transforming the feudal country his grandfather had ruled. Just before Hussein's advent to power, Abdullah had annexed the West Bank of the Jordan adding a foreign, agriculturally rich territory inhabited by Palestinians to his desert holdings. In order to placate the relatively urbane and sophisticated Palestinians, as well as the growing number of Jordanian dissidents who resented the excessive British control over their country, Hussein terminated the overt British management of his country. Thereafter subsisting on the British subsidy and a similar one forwarded to him from the American Central Intelligence Agency, Hussein was able to consolidate his control over his country with the help of his loyal army, which some have referred to as a private militia.

The purpose to the creation of Jordan in the British calculation of their self-interest is to be found at least in part in the strategic importance of the Gulf of Eilat (Aqaba) at Jordan's southernmost point. From the Gulf of Eilat (Aqaba), British supplies arriving through the Suez Canal could be transported to Iraq and Iran. The addition of another British-oriented state in the region also went far to guarantee British hegemony over the region.

LEBANON AND SYRIA

The most significant feature of Lebanon, its ethnic diversity, underlies every aspect of its national existence—from its separation from Greater Syria, to its politics, economy, and armed forces. Ruled as a separate sanjaq under the Ottomans, owing to the predominance of the Christian Maronites in the commercial and cultural life of the country and the influence of the French on the Maronites, Lebanon became one of the four states fissioned off from Greater Syria following the awarding in 1920 of Syria to the French as a mandate by the League of Nations. At that time Greater Syria, which in the past was regarded as an integral unit, was divided into the Alawite state of Latakia, the state of Jebel Druze, the Syrian state proper with Damascus as its capital, and Lebanon. Owing to the ethnic, cultural, and religious diversity of these four regions, there had traditionally been a great deal of enmity between the peoples inhabiting the newly divided states. The intent, however, was the old imperialist dictum of divide and rule, and particularly, to take advantage of the commercial edge maintained by the Maronites of Lebanon.

As the patrons of the economically dominant group, the French imposed a ubiquitous superstructure over the gerrymandered mandate. The Lebanese state, for example, was drawn exactly in a way to preserve the economic supremacy of the Maronites within borders in which the primarily Moslem peasantry was subordinated. The Maronites and the landed Sunni were united by economic interests in a state fissioned along European lines, which guaranteed the French important ports and a springboard for further penetration in the Middle East.

As for Syria, its heterogeneous citizenry was kept acutely aware of its sectarian differences by the French mandatory government. In 1925, however, an uprising originating in Jebel Druze spread throughout the country in violent opposition to the French rule. As a result, the states of Allepo and Damascus were united in a Syrian state. In 1937 similar protestations resulted in the unification of Latakia with Jebel Druze and reintegration of all the segments of Greater Syria, with the exception of Lebanon, under Allied occupation in 1942. In 1941 Lebanon was declared independent, although the actual departure of foreign troops was not effected until 1945. This independence guaranteed that the French would be able to benefit from a strategic base in the Middle East that was strongly allied with France, culturally and religiously. This enabled the Allies to facilitate a process leading to the reunification and independence of Greater Syria beginning in 1942, which was finally effected through the withdrawal in 1946 of foreign troops. The two and a half decades of French mandate had given the leading families of the various Syrian substates the opportunity to fortify their capital formations. The departure of the Allies in 1946 left Syria in the control of the newly consolidated bourgeoisie, who had declared a Syrian republic in which they would be dominant, in order to preserve their economic standing. Since the creation of the Syrian republic, the legitimizing creed in the country has been pan-Arabism.

Awarded varying degrees of autonomy, Syria remained, until well after its establishment in 1946, a state greatly dependent on the French. A series of treaties were more or less foisted on the Syrians, granting France a privileged position with respect to commerce, monetary matters, military facilities, and other resources. Since its independence, Syria has suffered one change in government after another, virtually all of which were accomplished through force. The present tottering rule of President Hafez al-Assad holds the record for governmental stability in Syria. It is significant to note, however, that Assad is an unadulterated dictator and that his regime is facing grave threats from political, religious, and ethnic dissidence within the country.

Until the civil war of 1975-76, Lebanon functioned politically as a liberal democracy with political power following those with economic clout; these economic leaders were primarily the Maronites and some elements of the Sunni sector. The confessional system guaranteed that the unspoken "National Pact" by which the various communities in the country knew their political caste and economic class served as the sole underpinning for the society. With the Civil War the system collapsed, and the uneasy lull that has endured in the country since that time represents a vacuum between the old system and a new Lebanese identity that promises to be very different from the old.

EGYPT AND SUDAN

Of all the Arab countries presently under discussion, Egypt is the most homogenous with respect to language, religion, and ethnicity. Next to Lebanon, it is also the Arab country with the longest history of European involvement. Its government and place in the Middle East has been greatly shaped by the European penetration into the country.

Initially, the European interest in Egypt rested in its strategic location as the frontispiece of three continents. With the construction of the Suez Canal, the country became even more important as a maritime asset to the imperial powers of Europe. Although the company owning the Canal was French, it fell under increasing British influence and virtual ownership with the occupation of Egypt by Britain in 1882. The creation of a joint British-Egyptian condominium over the Sudan provided an important bonus to the British presence in the area. The Nile basin was increasingly utilized in the development of plantations and agricultural industries that would benefit Britain economically. Exemplifying this was the diversion of Nile waters from farmlands in the Egyptian south to British plantations in the Sudan, where cotton destined for English textiles factories was grown.

Although Egypt received varying degrees of independence in the period from 1922 through World War II, the British involvement in the country was pronounced until the 1952 Free Officer's Coup. The British, through a direct presence and later through expansive treaty provisions, exercised a virtual carte blanche in Egypt and the Sudan, especially with respect to the utilization of the country as a transit and communications base for its military. It is against this backdrop that the relative militancy of Egypt at its most decisive hour was achieved under President Gamal Abdul Nasser. Nasser provided the Egyptian masses with a revolution opposed to Western imperialism in their country, and it was this "negative" nationalism that allowed Egypt to emerge fully as an independent state at the forefront of the Third World movement.

Saudi Arabia

The history of Saudi Arabia since the downfall of the Hashemite Kingdom of the Hejaz in 1922 is inextricably linked to the fortunes of the Saudi family. The Saudis, formerly the rulers of the Arabian interior, the Nedj, were the repository for the temporal prowess of the Wahhabi Islamic puritancial movement of eighteenth and nineteenth century Arabia. The Saudis, who were desert warriors fighting under the standard of the late King Faisel, have since converted their huge desert into a state with all the technological innovations of advanced western countries. The country remains, however, the private fiefdom of the Saudi family, in whom all decision making is vested. There is a socioeconomic stratification as well, with imported Palestinian and Yemini labor undertaking the menial tasks of the daily building that characterizes the country.

With the discovery of petroleum deposits in the Persian Gulf area of the country during the mid-1930s, the Saudis gradually became treasured by the West. Despite its dictatorial and nonrepresentative character, Saudi Arabia has been appeased because it is fabulously rich in oil. In reality, the Saudi family is the state. There is no other legitimizing agent in Saudi Arabia, and any changes in the status quo due to labor disaffection, religious unrest, or external threat bodes badly for the longevity of the country as presently constituted.

The Persian Gulf Sheikdoms

The Persian Gulf sheikdoms—Oman, Qatar, Bahrain, Kuwait, and the United Arab Emirates—have, for the most part, sustained a single form of government over the last two centuries: the feudal, authoritarian form of patriarchy had been frozen in time since the British recognition and de facto support for the rulers over the last 200 years. Through truces, protective treaties, and other forms of support, the British had gone a long way to insure that the ruling elites of today are continuous with the power centers that ruled the countries at the outset of the European imperial penetration of the Middle East.

Kuwait, the wealthiest of the Persian Gulf sheikdoms and one of the most technologically sophisticated countries in the world, exists primarily on the revenues of its petroleum resources. The country is the private estate of the Sabah family, which has ruled the country since 1710, prior to the conclusion of a treaty with the British in the late eighteenth century. Although over 50 percent of the inhabitants of Kuwait are immigrants who have no formal rights in the country, the Sabah clan has effectively consolidated its control over the country. This was achieved through disbursements on public projects and subsidization to its Arab neighbors through the Kuwaiti Fund for Arab Economic Development to deter any internal or external opposition to its rule. Also, the facade of democracy maintained by the Sabahs has resulted in the election of a Legislative Assembly. The assembly, however, functions solely for the benefit of the "native" Kuwaitis, who constitute a minority elite in the country.

Similarly, Bahrain is the realm almost exclusively of the al-Khalifa family, which gained control of the country in 1783 from the Iranians. Afterward, Bahrain entered into a protective status under the British, which was formalized in 1820. Likewise, the present ruling regime in Qatar, the Al Thani family, won control over this peninsula in the late 1860s after the British intervened on their behalf. While small in number, the population of the state is virtually coextensive with the Al Thani family.

Like the other Persian Gulf statelets, Qatar is what it is today due to British assistance and later to its oil revenues. Almost identical in history to Bahrain and Qatar are the sheikdoms that together comprise the United Arab Emirates, a state that did not achieve independence until 1971. While there has been a number of violent changes in rulers, the emirates are basically in the hands of the power centers that have governed the area since the eighteenth century. In some of the sheikdoms, the native population is a minority compared to the number of immigrants who have arrived recently. The latter's political and economic rights in the country are minimal to nil. Likewise, Oman, a sultanate in which the Abu Sa'id family, which has ruled Oman since 1749, has its fortunes today due to British protection of its dynasty and to its enriched coffers, owing to the infusion of petrodollars.

The rule of the Ziyadi Imamate, a religious form of government, had dominated Yemen for nearly a millenium until the Anglo-Turkish Convention of 1914 divided the country between an Ottoman northern sphere and a British protectorate in the south. Traditionally the most independent of the Arab polities, Yemen and southern Yemen had been beset by ongoing hostility between power centers and by superpower rivalry between the British, the Italians, and previously the Ottomans. Influence over Yemen was an important asset for the British in their campaign to win control over the Middle East; indeed it was something for which they battled mightily in order to secure undisputed strategic dominance over both outlets to the Indian Ocean through the Suez to the Bab al-Mandeb, that is, from the Persian Gulf to the Arabian Sea.

The demise of the Ottoman Empire, the entry of the European powers onto the Middle Eastern stage and the replacement of direct European control with indigenous power centers comprise the foundation on which contemporary Arab government is based. To argue that the Arab states were established in response to the needs and desires of the Arab masses is to ignore the historical realities that shaped Middle Eastern affairs over the last two centuries.

The highly centralized, authoritarian nature that characterizes Middle East society today is an imperative of contemporary Arab governments. Only through the imposition of totalitarian regimes and the perpetuation of feudal-styled political monarchies can the cliques in control of the Arab states continue their rule. In an age where literacy has brought democratic values to the commoner, the belief that the Arab regimes can continue their deprivation of civil liberties and human rights to their respective citizenries will lead to increased indigenous opposition. Gradual change through reform or dramatic alteration of existing institutions through revolution are the only alternatives to the continued repression in the Arab world.

The transfer of wealth from the industrialized West to the treasuries of the Arab ruling elites may, as some have asserted, be rectifying a historical injustice. However, the diversion of this oil wealth and its concentration in the hands of the Arab ruling elites neither serves to better the lot of the Arab commoner nor to erase injustice from the region. Only by the application of elementary democratic principles and procedures will contemporary governments in the Middle East fulfill their mission.

4

FROM FEUDALISM TO PETRODOLLARS:
THE MIDEAST TRANSFORMED

The role of economics in shaping the contemporary Middle East has been a preeminent one. The transformation of the Middle East from Ottoman feudalism to its present status as the fulcrum of global economic affairs can be comprehended only by analyzing the historical processes that have gone into the molding of the region over the past century. Of these historical processes, the emergence of oil as a key component of modern industry, transportation, and agriculture has been the element with the greatest impact on the evolution of the Middle East. The unique structure of the Middle East-based oil industry has directly determined political and social developments in the region. Accordingly, there cannot be a suitable redefinition of the Middle East coherent with the region's underlying realities without undertaking a thorough account of the origins, organization, and power of Middle East oil.

An analysis of the role played by Middle East oil in influencing social and political phenomena in the region requires a description of Ottoman feudalism and the demise of the Ottoman Empire. Oil has become strategically important only since World War I. There are historical antecedents extending into the eighteenth and nineteenth centuries that paved the way for the manipulation of Middle East resources by the European imperial powers and by the Western oil companies. The significance of the strategic waterways and of indigenous resources and products in the penetration of the region by the imperial powers potentiated the emergence of Middle East oil power.

OTTOMAN FEUDALISM

The socioeconomic basis of the Ottoman Empire was a feudal one similar in many of its aspects to European feudalism. The stratification and structuring of Ottoman society had as its purpose the perpetuation of Ottoman suzerainty in the political, cultural, and economic spheres. The assumption by the Ottoman sultanate of the caliphate added to the mystification enjoyed by the Ottoman authorities. To insure that the Ottomans maintained their position, a stratified system of economic and military structures was established in the Middle East.

At the height of the Ottoman Empire, the sultanate was protected by the Jannasaries, an elite corp of Christian fighting slaves. Within the Sublime Porte, officials drawn from the slave classes and from the Moslem free-borns carried out their functions under the supervision of the grand vizier, who was the effective instrument of government appointed and ruled by the grace of the sultan. In the field, further from the seat of Ottoman power, the Ottoman authority was exercised through a network of lords, who enforced Ottoman policy as they pleased. This class of lords were, in effect, the landowners of the vast areas over which they ruled. Given the degree of autonomy they enjoyed, they governed their fiefdoms as they wished. Consequently, the damage incurred by excessive taxation depended on the greed of the individual lord.

By the eighteenth century, however, the entire Ottoman machine began to collapse. The feudal lords became increasingly uninterested in the affairs of the sultanate. Huge estates, which served as tax farms, were created over which the former servants of the empire ruled. The empire began a process of fragmentation with only nominal allegiance paid to the sultanate. Communal differences were asserted throughout the Ottoman realm, and non-Ottoman traditional modes of rule, all of them feudal in structure, operated and created a kind of loose association of ethnonational, linguistic, and religious subgroups. Bedouins became less subject to Ottoman dictates, which they defied by resorting to their time-honored tribal organization. In the areas inhabited by sedentary Arabs, the power of the sheiks and mukhtars reemerged. The Druze were once again subservient to their foremost families, including, for example, the Jumblats of southern Lebanon. Among the Kurds, new ruling families came forward and asserted control over Kurdistan according to the age-old, pre-Ottoman style. The payment of tribute to the sultan continued on a sporadic and arbitrary basis. Consequently, the strength of the Ottoman sultan waned considerably.

There were multiple economic undercurrents that interacted and weakened the imperial dynasty. Among these was the circumnavigation of Africa, which permitted maritime Europe to trade directly with Asia. Concurrently, the European colonial powers began to use the Mediterranean and the Fertile Crescent as a transit station for the overland transport of supplies and commodities between Europe and the East. This strategic significance of the Middle East as a way station toward India and the other colonies in the East would remain strong through World War II. At this time the strategic importance of the region changed but by no means weakened.

Another factor that assisted in the loosening of the Ottoman hold over the Middle East was, ironically, the strengthening of trade between Europe and the Middle East. The primary European partner in this trade was France, which had started modest commerce with the region in the sixteenth century. This trade was basically restricted to the Mediterranean areas of the empire; the hinterland of the empire was not directly affected by it. The imports to the region were primarily consumer goods such as clothing and hardware, as well as metals and other items of relative luxury. Obviously the only class to benefit from this trade was the Ottoman aristocracy. On the other hand, the Levant exported fibers and a few crops. Among the fibers, the most important was cotton. Silk, cultivated in Lebanon, was also exported to Europe to the economic benefit of the Maronite and Druze feudal lords.

As a result of the global dislocations induced by the eruption of the U.S. Civil War, the Ottoman Empire was able to fill its coffers and stay intact for its final decades, largely due to the increased demand for tobacco, grown in Anatolia, and cotton, which was cultivated in the Sudan and Egypt. Eventually, British production and marketing interests would benefit considerably from the cultivation of the superior Egyptian strain of cotton. The unification of the Sudan with Egypt served the British cotton estates in the Sudan, which benefited from the diversion of Nile water at the expense of the southern Egyptian farmers.

The overall effect of trade with the Ottomans was of fluctuating value to the Europeans. It did serve, however, to maintain the cultural ties between the Levant and Europe, and this contact served to inculcate Western nationalist notions within the budding Arab intelligentsia of the late nineteenth century. This cultural bridge had been extended by the Napoleonic foray into Egypt and Palestine at the beginning of the nineteenth century. In the aftermath of the invasion, British and French trading and banking concerns were established in Egypt and other Mediterranean areas. This led the various rulers of the Middle East to an increasing dependence on the British and French economic interests. The result was often bankruptcy for the native concerns, due to the inept management of state affairs by the local autocrats. On the pretext of seizing assets to cover losses sustained by private European companies, the governments of France, England, and Italy occupied Tunis in 1881, Egypt in 1882, and Morocco in 1912.

The takeover of these countries cannot, of course, be attributed solely to the default of payments by the native monarchs to the Europeans. There were wider issues involved, and these were mainly superpower rivalry over Middle Eastern strategic waterways and overland routes. Further, the capital intensification that went into the development of railroads, canals, and ports in the Middle East was entirely under the control of the Europeans, who systematically and rapidly advanced their influence over the region.

THE STRATEGIC WATERWAYS

There are three sets of strategic waterways. The first includes the Dardenelles, the Sea of Marmara, and the Bosphoros, which together connect the Black Sea with the Mediterranean. For much of the Ottoman reign over the Middle East, the Black Sea was a "Turkish lake," which the Sublime Porte controlled. The outlets into the Black Sea were toll stations that provided the Porte with a greatly needed source of revenue. Eventually, Russia gained permission to sail through the outlets unencumbered by Ottoman taxation, and this privilege was later granted to peaceful maritime activity of ships sailing under other flags.

The control over the Black Sea and, of necessity, over its outlets became a strategic objective of the Russians, which would motivate much of their policy and activity with respect to the Ottoman Empire. A series of eighteenth and nineteenth century treaties came into force, alternately granting Russia special rights in the sea and its outlets and later blocking these special rights. The reversals came about as a result of British pressure on the Ottomans. The Russian expansionist policy southward threatened the British, since the latter were busily attempting to enhance their strategic and economic interest in the Middle East.

With the formation of the Entente bloc, which included both Britain and Russia during World War I, the British agreed to Russian control over both sets of straits assuming, of course, that there was an Entente victory. In actuality, the postwar settlements did not place the Sea of Marmara and the straits exclusively under Soviet control. The treaties of Lausanne and Montreaux provided a new legal definition according to which the sea and the straits were considered the joint possession of the Black Sea community of states.

The second strategic waterway is the Suez Canal/Bab al-Mandeb unit, between which is the Red Sea that is fed by the Gulf of Eilat (Aqaba). The Bab al-Mandeb is that stretch of water between Africa and Arabia where the Red Sea empties into the Indian Ocean. Prior to the building of the Suez Canal, the Red Sea/Bab al-Mandeb area played an important, but inherently limited, role in trade between Europe and the East. While cargo could be carried to Arabia and Africa over water, trade with the East proceeded overland. The Suez Canal directly connected the Mediterranean Sea and the Indian Ocean and thereby effectively linked the West to the East.

The construction of the Suez Canal came at the midpoint between the European penetration of the region following Napoleon's invasion of Egypt and the dismantlement of the Ottoman Empire. Its construction—indeed, the entire European economic initiative in the region—was both a cause of and a beneficiary of waning Ottoman strength. In the short run, however, there was an infusion of capital into the sultan's treasury deriving from the revenues generated by the French purchase of the canal concession. By the early 1880s, though, the British had not only managed to financially dislodge the Ottomans, but also the French, thereby becoming the economic masters of the invaluable Suez Canal waterway. This economic hegemony led to the British occupation of Egypt in 1881.

The creation of the Suez Canal was the brainchild of Ferdinand de Lesseps, a French official stationed in Egypt, who utilized a friendship with the Ottoman viceroy of Egypt to obtain a concession for the Canal. Although the concession was granted in 1854, it was not until 1869 that the canal itself was completed. The delay was due as much to British efforts to frustrate their rivals, the French, as to the technological problems confronting the building of the waterway.

The canal was to be constructed and owned by the Compagnie Universalle du Canal Maritime Suez, according to a concession that accorded a 99 year lease to the company. After the termination of the concession, the ownership of the canal was to be vested in the hands of the Ottoman government in Egypt. In the interim, the Ottoman government was to receive 15 percent of the company's yearly profit.

Given the deteriorating status of the Egyptian viceroyalty, the British were able in 1875 to purchase the 15 percent of company stock owned by the Ottoman government in Egypt. While the company remained dominated by the French shareholders, various domestic upheavals in Egypt gave the British the pretext they needed to occupy the country and consequently gain effective control over the canal. The occupation of the canal zone, and of Egypt and the Sudan in general, gave a boost to Britain's accelerating industrialization. Cotton farming in the southern part of Egypt and in the Sudan, as well as the advantage of direct shipping afforded by the canal, benefited the British economy considerably. The control over the canal gave the British an unprecedented concentration of economic power in the East. The strategic value of the canal and of the entire Bab al-Mandeb unit greatly enhanced Britain's Eastern policy. Britain retained control or enjoyed privileges concerning the canal throughout the period that ended only after Gamal Abdul Nasser nationalized the canal in 1956.

The Persian Gulf/Straits of Hormuz/Gulf of Oman strategic unit is the third of the Middle East's strategic waterways. The Tigris and Euphrates rivers going deep into Mesopotamia feed into the Persian Gulf. The primary significance of the unit in the period before the petroleum age was basically restricted to trade and strategic functions. This trade, involving the lands of what is now Iraq, Syria, Saudi Arabia, the Trucial States, Yemen, and Iran, took place in an area that traditionally straddled the trade routes between the hinterlands of the Middle East and the Far East. The increase of European trade with the region and the growth of the imperial chains between Europe and the East made the area an important staging and supply area for the European powers. The maritime unit was a key link in the communications, transportation, and trade routes between Europe and the Middle East, Europe and the Far East, and the Middle East and the Far East.

EUROPEAN IMPERIALISM'S MIDEAST APPROACH

The increasing importance of oil in the global economy, and the location of rich oil fields in the Persian Gulf area, increasingly made the area a center of economic power. The waterways have assumed an expanded significance since they are the channels by which oil is transported out of the area. The waterways have become objects of disputes and contested claims, as exemplified, for example, by the conflicts between Iran, Iraq, and Abu Dabai over the three Persian Gulf islands of the Greater and Lesser Tunbs and Abu Musa. Their location in the Persian Gulf area abutting the Straits of Hormuz makes them the key to the control of traffic into and out of the Persian Gulf.

For most of the past two centuries, Britain has had almost complete control over the lands and governments of the southern and eastern littorals of the Arabian Peninsula. Consequently, they held a considerable strategic advantage over the traffic that went in and out of the area and this, of course, provided them with preferential terms for their trade and interests. The countries of eastern Arabia, including today's United Arab Emirates, as well as Qatar and Oman, were covered under the treaty of protection arrived at with Britain in the eighteenth and nineteenth centuries. Similarly, the British imperialist interests and those of the Kuwaiti sheiks benefited from the symbiotic relationship with the British. The parameters of this relationship were such that Britain maintained the governments of individuals with whom they were aligned, in return for cooperation in the granting of favorable strategic and economic conditions to Britain. This was enhanced by the creation of a similar treaty between Britain and Aden and complemented by the Russo-Anglo division of Iran during

World War I. British influence was evident throughout the interwar era, when many of the British protectorates and principalities obtained statehood. With the involvement of United States' and, to a much lesser extent, European and Japanese oil companies in the area, the frequency of use, the development, and political nature of the Persian Gulf area was significantly altered. These changes followed the economic transformation that the area underwent as a result of the windfall petroleum revenues.

The backdrop against which Middle East oil emerged as a powerful economic force in the twentieth century is the European imperial penetration of the region throughout the nineteenth century. The characteristics of this penetration began as a strategic necessity of the various European empires. The Middle East was not initially viewed so much as an objective in itself but more as a transit and communications way station to the East.

The increasing significance of trade with the Middle East, which gave the European powers a new source of resources and markets during the nineteenth century, enhanced the importance of the region to the British, French, Italian, Germans, and Russians. To protect this trade as well as the strategic routes to the East, the strategic waterways in the region grew in importance. The construction of the Suez Canal, though initially unjustified in terms of the amount of trade then transpiring between Europe and the Middle East, became a significant imperial objective during the course of the decade it took to construct the canal. Eventually its strategic importance became more apparent to the British and the French, with the former successfully winning control over the canal.

Aside from the strategic waterways, the other means utilized by the imperial powers to entrench themselves in the region include the facilitation and protection of private European commercial concerns in the region. Given the corrupt and ineffectual leadership of the various lands in the region during the final decades of Ottoman decay, European commercial concerns were able to impose a dependence on the despots controlling the treasuries of the various Middle East lands. The chicanery and ability employed by the Europeans to manipulate the inexperience of the indigenous despots enabled the European commercial concerns to bankrupt the various countries in which they were involved. All of these business dealings were accompanied by the energetic involvement of "political agents" dispatched by the European countries to protect their interests in the region. Following the bankruptcy of the various countries, the Europeans entered the region by direct force in order to safeguard their interests in the Middle East.

The third tactic employed by the Europeans to consolidate their control over the Middle East involved the achievement of numerous "treaties of protection," by which the imperial powers supported various indigenous power centers in their effort to capture and maintain their rule over their respective fiefdoms. In exchange for this "protection," the European powers, most notably the British, were given freedom to pursue their interests in the region. The primary area of activity in which "protection treaties" were operative was eastern Arabia, which was ruled in accordance with the policies of the European colonial offices, although it was under the nominal suzerainty of local rulers.

The dates during which indigenous power centers became appendages of European imperial design are as follows: Oman first entered formal relations with the British through a trade agreement in 1839. The trade agreement was extended into a protection treaty in 1891, which led to the "Indianization" of Oman within the British Empire. The British control over Oman continued well into the post-World War II period, and the involvement of Britain in engineering native government according to its interests was considerable. The country has subsequently been consolidated under the control of the Arab sultanate that continues to rule the country. Ethnonational and linguistic differences between the Ethiopic Dhofari population of Oman and the Perso-Arabic Omanis proper have been submerged beneath a pan-Arabic legitimizing creed.

The sheiks of what is today known as the United Arab Emirates signed their treaty of friendship with the British in 1820. The agreement is known as the General Treaty of Peace, and it remained in effect up to the independence of the United Arab Emirates in 1971. The presently ruling al-Sabah family of Kuwait first signed their treaty with the British in 1899. The British were interested in assisting the renegade al-Sabah clan because German designs on Kuwait as a terminus for the Berlin-Baghdad railroad threatened British hegemony in the gulf area. Bahrain, whose present rulers, the Khalifa family, have been the controlling dynasts of the country for the past two centuries, entered into a relationship with Britain in 1820. The country's population is a mixture of Arabs, Persians, Sunnis, and Shiites. Britain maintained direct influence over the country until its independence in 1971.

Another Persian Gulf state "protected" by treaty with the British was Qatar. Finally, northern Yemen, the linchpin of the Bab al-Mandeb strategic unit was won over to British control gradually throughout the nineteenth century. Over time, a mutually beneficial and brisk commercial trade relationship was transformed into British colonial control over northern Yemen. The latter was perceived as an imperative of British imperialism in order to guard British holdings in the East.

HEGEMONY BY DISMANTLEMENT OR COOPTATION

Recognition of the inherent and strategic value of the Middle East by the European powers began, basically, in the late nineteenth century. At that time two strategies emerged for the achievement of imperial hegemony over the region. The first of these, maintained by Britain, France, Russia, and Italy involved the dismantlement of the Ottoman Empire, which was already in an advance stage of decline. The other strategy, that of the Germans, involved the strengthening of the Ottoman Empire and its utilization as a puppet regime.

Both colonial strategies, however, shared basic approaches toward the attainment of influence. First, the creation of dependent commercial relationships between European concerns and the various dynasts who were then governing led to the assumption of direct control by the Europeans over the lands of the defaulting Middle East rulers. Secondly, European development of Middle East transit and communications routes (for example, the Suez Canal, the Berlin-Baghdad railroad, etc.) eventually led to the contest, won by the Entente powers after World War I, for the administration of the countries adjacent to the strategic waterways. Thirdly, European colonialism was riveted by a series of treaties and pacts between elites and the European powers. It is upon this colonial foundation that the power of Middle East oil was generated.

THE RACE FOR PETROLEUM RESOURCES

Although the first production of petroleum in the Middle East began during the 1870s in Baku, in what is presently Soviet Azerbaijan, the real age of Middle East oil began with the obtainment of a concession to drill for oil in Persia in 1901 by the British gold magnate William Knox D'Arcy. The D'Arcy concession exemplifies both the beginnings of the importance of oil in the economy of the industrializing West and the manner in which Western oil companies chose to develop a relationship with the peoples and resources of the Middle East.

Generally, the history of petroleum production began with the creation of a U.S. company, John D. Rockefeller's Standard Oil of New Jersey, to extract and refine oil in the United States. At the time, the uses of petroleum were confined to medicinal products and kerosene, and the United States served as the world's biggest producer of these commodities. D'Arcy became interested in oil production after observing the relative ease with which his fellow plutocrat, Rockefeller, was able to extract a fabulous wealth from his petroleum holdings. As oil became increasingly important to modern technologi-

cal innovations such as the automobile, D'Arcy turned his attention
to the fuel as a new source of fortune.

D'Arcy was not, however, the only Britisher to recognize the
economic importance that petroleum was to play in the rapidly industrializing West. While it took him a decade to convince his government of the importance of oil, D'Arcy's economic concern soon became a British imperial interest. Even before Britain's official and
financial involvement in the oil exploration business, it had facilitated
cooperation between its official petroleum company, Burmah Oil, and
D'Arcy's concern. With the near collapse of D'Arcy company, the
British government assisted in the formation of the Anglo-Persian
Oil Company, which exploited a concession granted to D'Arcy by the
Qajar rulers in Tehran.

The business of finding and exploiting the oil concession in Iran
proved formidable in several ways. The concession granted to D'Arcy
by the Qajar shah covered land in the Khuzestan province of the country, in Iran's southwest. Khuzestan's significance as an oil-producing
and strategic area of the Persian Gulf is well known, as illustrated by
Iraq's invasion and occupation of the province in 1980. Khuzestan is
not only the source of much of Iran's oil reserves, but the Shaat al-
Arab estuary where the Tigris and Euphrates flow into the Persian
Gulf is also found in the province. While Khuzestan is very much an
Arab land demographically (the Arab inhabitants of the area and the
Arab states refer to the district as Arabestan, "land of the Arabs"),
its traditional rulers included the sheiks and khans of the Bakhtiari,
a people related to the Kurds and distinct from the Persians and Arabs
of the region.

The resistance of the Bakhtiaris to the entrance of the British
oil prospectors into their region complicated the concession agreement between the D'Arcy company and the central government in Tehran. The latter exercised little control over the fiercely independent
Bakhtiaris, who demanded the payment of a royalty not foreseen or
stipulated in the original concession agreement. Since the Bakhtiaris
were more the rulers of Khuzestan than were the Qajars of Tehran,
D'Arcy was forced to acquiesce to their demand for paying a royalty.
In a precedent-setting act of chicanery that would characterize the
future dealings of oil companies with the peoples of the Middle East,
D'Arcy paid the Bakhtiaris their royalty but deducted the amount from
the royalty owed to the Qajar treasury. It is this kind of practice that
helped make the Western oil companies so tremendously wealthy, while
also infuriating the indigenous populations by their nefarious business
practices. Sensing the possible danger that confronted the D'Arcy concern from the disgruntled Khuzestani population, the Bengali Lancers,
a crack regiment of the Indian government, was deployed to Khuzestan
in order to protect the oil concern.

The initial failures faced by the D'Arcy company proved financially costly. Concurrently, news reached London of the impending conversion by the German navy from coal to the more efficient oil fuel. As tensions mounted between the two imperial powers on the eve of World War I, Winston Churchill, then first lord of the British Admiralty, sought ways by which the D'Arcy concern could be supported. The formation of Anglo-Persian was one of the methods utilized to expand the capital of the British concern in Persia. In this concern, the public Burmah Oil Company was a major shareholder along with D'Arcy. However, Churchill sought to expand Britain's role in the increasingly important oil enterprises of the Middle East. He therefore introduced a bill to the House of Commons calling for the purchase by the British Government of 51 percent of Anglo-Persian stock. While this would give the British government a controlling interest in the company, Churchill had reached agreement with the company's directors indicating that complete control of the day-to-day operations of the enterprise would remain in the hands of the private shareholders. From the company's point of view, an infusion of capital for the construction of refinery facilities and pipelines was necessary. A residual benefit of the British government's involvement in the firm was the additional resources that became available to the firm. Among these, diplomatic and military support as well as financial assistance were included.

From the British government's vantage point, its involvement in the production of petroleum resources was becoming more and more a strategic necessity. Further, as the major shareholder in the company, the British military would benefit from preferential terms and advantageous supplies of petroleum. This in turn fed back most favorably into the British economic situation: the British navy and airforce were guaranteed all necessary supplies of oil fuel at a discounted rate from the company. Therefore, not only did the British government benefit economically by saving on the cost of oil fuel going to its military, but the discounted rate at which the military bought the fuel also provided a nominal reduction in the company's profits. Since the Persian and Bakhtiari rulers were being remunerated according to a royalty schedule based on profit rather than on the quantity of oil produced from their land, their royalty was calculated on the basis of the company's apparent loss of revenue. While the Persians and Bakhtiaris were receiving less in oil royalties, the company gained by not having to pay this expenditure. All the while, the British government, the dominant shareholder in the company, benefited by the reduction of the amount of royalty paid to the Middle East rulers, as well as by the discounted prices it paid to its own company for oil used by its military. The result was a loss of immediate revenue for the Persians and Bakhtiaris, as well as a long-term loss due to the depletion of the finite supply of oil. The British government benefited from reduced prices and expenditures and the private British stockholders also gained from the reduction of royalty payments.

The status quo continued throughout the war years with respect to the exploitation of oil resources in the Middle East. Anglo-Persian prospered with the de facto division of Iran into a southern zone dominated by the British and a northern zone, which was under Russian control. At the war's end, the Russian ability to control their zone of Iran weakened considerably as a result of the October Revolution, and the British became the de facto masters of the country. At the same time that Britain was extending its control over Iran, the French were contesting British designs in Mesopotamia and Syria. The French maintained that Britain's postwar strategy with respect to western Asia was based on petroleum considerations rather than on territorial issues, which was the basis of France's colonial policy. Concurrently, the Turkish authorities were challenging the armistice agreements, particularly with respect to Mesopotamia. As the allies and successor of the Germans in the region, the Turks argued that what they had previously ruled should remain theirs. The area under particular dispute was the Mosul area of Mesopotamia in Kurdistan. Turkish claims were based on the existence of the Berlin-Baghdad railroad, which ran through Kirkuk. The reason for this considerable diversion of the railroad by the indirect route leading through Kirkuk derived from the agreement reached between the Anatolian Railroad Company and the Ottomans. The former were entitled under the terms of the agreement to extract whatever mineral resources might be found in the area where the railroad was constructed. German engineers had detected the existence of petroleum reserves in the Kirkuk area, and consequently the Anatolian Railroad Company designed the railroad so that it would pass through the region. The minerals to be found there would, per agreement, be theirs to exploit. The Turks claimed Mosul as their own, on the legal grounds that they were the successor authority of the German/Turkish axis. The British countered by pointing out that the Turkish Petroleum Company, which controlled the modest exploitation of Mosul oil production, was a combine amalgamating British, German, Turkish, and Dutch interests in Mosul oil. The combine was divided into several blocs, with the British Anglo-Persian Oil Company holding the largest plurality of stock, specifically, 50 percent. The German Deutsche Bank held 25 percent, as did the mixed British/Dutch company, Dutch Shell. The British argued that, with the defeat of the Germans in the war, the portion owned by the Deutsche Bank was to be expropriated and, therefore, with the exception of the minor Dutch interest, Turkish Petroleum was for all practical purposes a British company.

Throughout the British/Turkish dispute, which eventually went to the League of Nations and the World Court for adjudication, the French played both sides against one another in order to maximize their eventual benefit. The Anglo-French agreement was achieved in a secret meeting that took place in 1919. The British were recognized as the rulers of Mosul, and in return for their accommodation and co-operation, the French were to receive a bloc of shares amounting to 25 percent in the Turkish Petroleum Company. Additionally, the British agreed to assist the French in the imposition of their control over Lebanon and Syria.

The British preoccupation with Mesopotamia, now called Iraq, was born of both strategic and economic causes. Lord Curzon, the chief architect of British imperial policy in the region, suggested that Persia and its gateway, Mesopotamia, were critical to British geo-strategic interests with respect to India and the colonies farther to the East. Additionally, Persian and increasingly Mesopotamian oil became assets in themselves. These objectives not only had to be pre-served for British control, but certainly they had to be kept from for-eign influence. Appropriate political administration of these imperial interests had to be attained, and to this objective British ingenuity ap-plied itself no less cleverly than it had in the economic and military spheres. This was accomplished in the artificial creation of the Iraqi state through a gradual process. First, the former Ottoman vilayets of Basra and Baghdad were conjoined, over which Britain was to re-ceive a mandate or full control and liberties, until such time as the country attained the political "maturity" to govern itself. After gain-ing the mandate and in preparation for the eventual transformation of the country from mandatory status to independence, the British hoped to gain a far-reaching treaty with the Iraqis by which they would con-trol those aspects of Iraq's policy that impinged on their strategic and economic interests.

In Persia, the arrangement for a suitable political entente be-tween the British and the central government came about as a result of the coup d'etat that ejected the pro-Soviet, anti-British administra-tion from office. The pro-Soviet tilt of the Iranian government came about largely in reaction to Britain's heavy-handed approach to a treaty it attempted to foist on the Iranians. The harsh tactics inflamed Iranian national sentiments and moved popular opinion toward the Soviets, with whom new oil concession agreements concerning territories in north-ern Iran were being negotiated. In the days just before the signing of an Iranian-Soviet friendship treaty, a coup by Western-oriented Iranian militarymen successfully placed a new, anti-Soviet regime into power. Among the inner clique of the revolutionaries was Reza Khan, who would later rise through the ranks of the new Iranian government to become minister of war and commander-in-chief. Reza eventually consolidated his control over Iran, to the extent of overthrowing his fellow revolutionaries as well as the figurehead Qajar Shah, and assuming the title of Shah-an-Shah of the new Pahlavi dynasty. Shah Reza was the father of Mohammed Reza Shah, the dictator of Iran until his deposal in 1979 at the hands of the Islamic revolutionaries.

Britain and Iran under the Pahlavis had a number of conflicts, all of which were resolved through negotiations. The central object of negotiations always returned to the terms of the Iranian national agreement with the Anglo-Iranian (formerly Anglo-Persian) Oil Company. Even if the clash concerned British flights to India through Iranian airspace or the replacement of capitulations to British nationals for some other quid pro quo, the underlying source of frustration was oil. A series of treaties formalized Britain's position in Persia throughout the interwar period.

THE WESTERN OLIGOPOLY OVER MIDEAST OIL

One of the conditions by which Britain was awarded the Iraqi mandate by the League of Nations was the so-called Open-Door Agreement, which guaranteed the freedom of non-British economic concerns to engage in business and development in Iraq. The British were, however, quite concerned about preserving their control over Iraq, and particularly over its oil. In the interim, a number of U.S. oil companies backed by Washington attempted to gain concessions from the Iraqi government. Therefore, Britain's nominal commitment to the Open-Door Agreement clashed with its imperial concerns. A quid pro quo was achieved by which the British shared the Turkish Petroleum Company with the U.S. companies. Consequently, in 1928, the Near East Development Company was formed, which was jointly owned by Standard Oil of New Jersey and Standard Oil Company of New York (Socony). This joint firm received a 23.75 percent share of the Turkish Petroleum Company, as did Anglo-Persian and the French Compagnie Francaise des Petroles. The remaining stock was held by a private shareholder.

With the national diversification of the Turkish Petroleum Company, the major Western oil companies benefited under the economic and political conditions pioneered by the Anglo-Persian Oil Company and the British government. The puppet regime of King Faisel in Iraq served superbly to insure the functioning of the interests of those companies that owned Turkish Petroleum. The ancillary benefits that accrued were the main pillars supporting the government of King Faisel and his successors in the Jordanian Hashemite dynasty.

The new marriage of the U.S. and European oil companies resulted in concerted, or at least coordinated, policies. One of the more important of these was the Red Line Agreement, which was conceived and agreed to by the representatives of the companies in July 1928. The agreement called for the consent and/or participation of all of the cooperating companies in the exploitation of oil wealth within the confines of the former Ottoman Empire.

The Red Line Agreement maximized the "horizontal integration" of the oil industry, by which the companies agreed to cooperate closely with one another to control the industry on a global scale. The agreement provided for an oligopoly in the production of oil within all Ottoman holdings, including the Arabian Peninsula, but excluding Bahrain and Kuwait, which Britain hoped to exploit by itself. There are, however, several different stages of production in the petroleum industry, with actual extraction of the product from subterranean pools being but one of these stages. Production, that is, the actual locating, drilling, and pumping of oil is, along with the second stage of the industry, refining, the most capital intensive of all phases. After production and refining comes the marketing stage, which entails the distribution of the various petroleum products (oil, gas, kerosene, diesel fuel, etc.). The latter stage is far more lucrative, since it involves very little capital. Further, the oligopic nature of the Western oil industry reduced competition between the companies to a minimum. This is to their advantage, since without the vagaries of competition, the companies, while working in concert, are free to arbitrarily set the price of petroleum products. Until the unilateral price-setting policies of the oil-producing countries came into effect in the early 1970s, there was only a small relationship between market forces and the price of petroleum: the companies were free to set whatever price they desired for the increasingly critical commodity.

The way the oligopoly of the petroleum industry is preserved is by the cooperation of the companies in such a way that they function as a virtual monopoly. All that it would take, however, to undermine this most lucrative and mutually beneficial business arrangement would be for one of the major companies to break from the cooperative framework and cut the highly inflated prices set by the informal cartel. This is prevented, however, by the high degree of "vertical integration" in the oil industry. The constituent companies of the oligopoly cooperate with one another concerning production, but each individual company maintains an integrated set of stages in the producing, refining, transporting, and marketing stages of the product. Therefore, if a maverick or independent company were to produce oil it would be left without a market, since the market is controlled by the competing companies in the oil-consuming countries. Vertical integration permits the companies to control both production and marketing and thereby preserve the cartelization of the oil industry. The petroleum company giants are concerned with preserving the profits of the company as a whole; if they must modify costs of any of the individual stages of oil production, this cost can be dissipated by a price hike at another stage of the production process. This is a matter of great import in explaining the oil crisis of the early 1970s.

Since production and marketing are different stages of the process, the oil companies had to supplement the Red Line production agreement with another relating to marketing. Therefore, the As-Is Agreement came into effect in 1928, by which the allocation of markets on a world scale were restricted by mutual agreement to the percentage of shares held by each country in the Iraq Petroleum Company.

With the consolidation of control by the Western oil companies over the Iraqi and Iranian markets, other horizons were sought by the companies as future sources of petroleum resources. The first of these appeared in Bahrain, the archipelago of islands in the Persian Gulf. A private British entrepreneur sold a concession he had received from the al-Khalifa family to Standard Oil of California (Socal), which despite its participation in the cartel managed to circumvent the letter of the cartel's law by forming an independent Canadian subsidiary, the Bahrain Petroleum Company (Bapco). This was accomplished despite the fact that the Bahrainis were virtually British puppets. The apparent disinterest of the Anglo-Persian in the profitability of drilling in Bahrain led them to veto IPCs involvement in that country. This opened the door for the creation of Bapco.

The creation of Bapco indicated the disadvantages that cartelization could cause the oil companies. As a result, a number of companies left the Iraq Petroleum Company so as not to be formally tied to the Red Line Agreement. As the focus of petroleum production shifted from Iraq and Iran to the Arabian peninsula, a new cartel was formed, one that was almost exclusively American. This process led to the Americanization of Middle East oil.

If oil could be found in Bahrain, it was assumed, then it could be found elsewhere in eastern Arabia, most probably in those areas closest to the Iraq/Iran proven reserves. The area was Kuwait, where Gulf Oil and Anglo-Persian formed a joint company (Kuwait Oil Company) to exploit Kuwaiti oil. The terms were most favorable to both concerns, since royalties negotiated with the al-Sabah family were less than those paid to the Iranians and to Iraq's Faisel. While the al-Sabahs received less royalty per barrel than the Shah and Faisel, the Kuwaitis were enriched beyond belief by the infusion of oil wealth. Kuwait had no infrastructure and relatively no economy until the formation of the Kuwait Oil Company. The production of oil in that country gave the sheik a veritable kingdom of fabulous wealth almost instantly. No other productive activity was necessary to make Kuwait the super economic power it has become. Accordingly, nothing other than capitulation to the treaty of protection with the British had been necessary for the al-Sabahs to maintain their control over the country.

The same logic dictating that if oil were to be found in Bahrain it could also be found in Kuwait led U.S. firms to drill for oil in Saudi Arabia. A U.S. company, the Arab American Oil Company (Aramco) was formed by Standard Oil of California and Texaco, Aramco was able to outbid Anglo-Persian for concessions in the private feifdom of Ibn Saud. The concessions were arranged by the U.S. Department of State in 1944 through an agreement providing Saudi Arabia with aid that would be forwarded directly to Ibn Saud. In other words, the oil concessions were bought for the Aramco (formerly Casco) by American subsidization of Ibn Saud.

On the eve of the Second World War, Middle East Oil was in the hands of the "seven sisters" or the "majors" as they have since become known. These companies, Texaco, Standard of New Jersey, Mobil, Gulf, Standard of California (all American companies), Anglo-Persian (now known as British Petroleum), and Royal Dutch Shell (now known as Shell, a mixed British/Dutch concern) maintained a virtual stranglehold on the industry. Despite their slow start, the American companies held 42 percent of the proven oil reserves in the Middle East on the eve of the Second World War. American governmental involvement with the affairs of the private American oil companies became a well-entrenched pattern not only during wartime, but throughout the post-World War II period as well. Not the least of these was the virtual nonpayment of taxes to the U.S. government, a benefit enjoyed by the oil companies due to their flair for creative accountancy, and the dovetailing of private economic interests with national strategic concerns.

The story of the oil wealth of the other Arabian states and sheikdoms greatly resembles that of Bahrain, Kuwait, and Saudi Arabia. Qatar, for example, derives approximately 95 percent of its wealth from oil, and of this up to 25 percent has gone directly to the sheik. The abuses of power and wealth in which the rulers of Oman and the sheikdoms of the United Arab Emirates have been engaged are awesome; often they were the product of deference paid to these rulers by the Western oil companies. The decadence of the elites ruling the newly created oil-producing states in the 1950s and 1960s was considerable. The exercise of their newly entrenched power brought authoritarian rule to their people, while at the same time giving Aramco a virtual carte blanche in their country.

In the 1950s, however, there emerged a growing consciousness on the part of the indigenous populations of Iran and Iraq concerning the great promise of the oil resources found in their lands. Along with this consciousness was the growing realization that, while their rulers were waxing rich as the partners of the ubiquitous and arrogant oil companies, the benefit of the newly found wealth was not filtering down to the people, nor was an adequate share of wealth and decision making being apportioned to the population as a whole.

THE STIRRINGS OF NATIONALIZATION

The first of these spontaneous upheavals against the exploitation of the oil resource by Western companies took place in Iran. This rebellion, led by the Iranian National Front party under the stewardship of the veteran Iranian nationalist Dr. Mohammed Mossadegh, had its roots in the overthrow of the Qajar dynasty. At that time a group of republicans had joined in the broadly-based movement to end the Qajar regime. When, however, Reza Khan declared himself Shah and proclaimed the rule of the Pahlavi dynasty, the republican elements were forced into opposition.

The British/Soviet occupation of Iran during the Second World War had been viewed by many of the nationalists not so much as part of the Allied campaign to arrest the spread of Nazi influence, but rather as an attempt by foreign powers to further exploit the country, particularly its oil resources. Against this backdrop, the National Front emerged, determined to have the government of Iran run by and in the interest of Iranians.

Following the termination of the occupation, during which Shah Reza was forced into exile and abdicated his throne in favor of his son, the late Shah Mohammed Pahlavi, social unrest merged with the agitation of the Tudeh Communist Party and the National Front, which demanded far-reaching reforms within the country. The young Shah's land reformation policies and development programs could not forestall the increased disaffection that pervaded Iran. The nationalists and communists were particularly effective in organizing the workers at the oil refineries and installations in Khuzestan and Abadan, and a series of strikes against Anglo-Iranian produced a number of work stoppages in the otherwise bonanza production of oil from the southwestern fields. The conditions under which the Iranian workers labored were disgraceful by any standard, and the nationalists seized upon that fact as an example of Iran's exploitation by the West.

Nationalist fervor ran high, and the Iranian legislative body, the Majlis, passed bills calling for minimum wages and workers' rights and benefits. The management of Anglo-Iranian refused to comply with the new laws, and this created a new symbol of Western exploitation of Iran in the minds of the populace of that country. The government under the Shah found the militancy of the workers threatening, and a series of crackdowns and repressive measures against the Tudeh party further fanned the already impassioned feelings of the citizenry. The Iranian masses had, with increasing vociferousness, thrown their support behind Dr. Mossadegh, who had emerged as a kind of national liberator attempting to break the yoke of foreign domination of his country. Mossadegh's efforts were viewed as having been encumbered by an effete, if not Western-oriented, puppet government led by the young Shah.

There was some abatement in the hostilities between the nationalists and the royalists when the latter expressed their outrage at British indications that they would send troops into Iran in order to insure continuing production in the oil fields. The nationalists' demands were unmollified by the Supplemental Agreement, which the British had put forward to the government. The agreement called for a considerable revision of the terms of the concession, in favor of Iran. The new government of Prime Minister Ali Razmara accepted the agreement, but the nationalists viewed the agreement as nothing but a minor reform in an inherently exploitive system. Unrest continued, not only in the oil-producing areas, but throughout the country's major cities. Demonstrations were rampant throughout Tehran, and the nationalists' demand for the nationalization of Anglo-Iranian became the war cry of the incensed Iranian citizenry. The country was becoming polarized into a small, isolated, but extremely powerful monarchist camp, which was backed by the Iranian military, and a large opposition bloc consisting of the outraged Iranian citizenry led by Mossadegh's National Front, and which operated in tacit cooperation with the Tudeh communists. In one sense, throughout 1950-51, there were two power centers ruling Iran: the monarchists and the military who controlled the country and its military, and Mossadegh who ruled the hearts and minds of the Iranian people.

The overt suppression against the nationalists was regarded as being both unseemly and counterproductive even after Prime Minister Razmara was assassinated by nationalist elements in March 1951. The nationalists were becoming increasingly brazen; a bill, which was symbolic of the scope of change they wished to introduce into the country, calling for the outright nationalization of Anglo-Iranian was introduced into the Majlis, which passed the bill into law.

Following the nationalization bill, indications that the British were prepared to exercise gunboat diplomacy were evident, particularly by the redeployment of British troops in the Mediterranean. The Iranian government fell during the ensuing crisis between the monarchists and the nationalists, and the Shah's recognition that he could only withstand the countervailing winds in his country by appeasing the nationalists prompted him to appoint Dr. Mossadegh prime minister, an appointment that was approved overwhelmingly by the Majlis in April 1951. Subsequently, the British moved more troops into the area and dispatched warships into the Persian Gulf. The obviously popular support that Mossadegh enjoyed motivated the British to use armed forces only as a last resort, and the Anglo-Iranian Company moved for arbitration of the original agreement. Dr. Mossadegh refused such arbitration, and the Iranians seized Anglo-Iranian holdings and renamed the company the National Iranian Oil Company (NIOC).

As a result of the nationalization, all production stopped at the

Khuzestan facilities. The British management refused to work under the direction of the National Iranian Oil Company officials, and the British threatened to sue or place a lien against the assets of any company or country accepting oil produced from Khuzestan under the NIOCs organization. The British threat did not prove an idle one. Additionally, Britain stepped up legal efforts at the International Court as well as diplomatic activities, which were negated by a single persuasive speech delivered by Mossadegh before the Security Council. Upon his return, in an effort to bring down the Shah, Mossadegh resigned his post as prime minister. This was followed within a week by the International Court of Justice's decision that it had no jurisdiction in the case, since it was an internal Iranian affair. In actuality this proved to be a boon for the Iranians.

Despite the solid political, judicial, and diplomatic grounds on which the Iranian nationalization rested, the internal structure of the petroleum industry with its horizontal integration and cartelization proved too formidable for the Iranian national campaign. The British had successfully enforced a boycott of Iranian oil, which had no detrimental effects at all for the profits of the companies. Since the majors controlled production throughout the Middle East, the suspension of oil production in Khuzestan, owing to the boycott of Iranian oil catalyzed Arabian production. Oil from Saudi Arabia, the Persian Gulf sheikdoms, Kuwait, and Qatar filled the gap introduced by the stoppage of Iranian production.

The change in U.S. administration led to a change of Washington's policy toward Mossadegh. Under Truman, considerable U.S. assistance went to Iran. With the assumption of power by President Eisenhower, a cooling, and eventually icing, of relations between Mossadegh and the U.S. administration took place. The United States was ostensibly fearful of the considerable power wielded by the Tudeh party in the affairs of Iran, and Mossadegh was angry about the U.S. refusal to step up assistance to his country. Between the suspension of oil production and the concomitant loss of revenues and the refusal of the U.S. government to fill the void, Iran was on the brink of economic bankruptcy. Under these conditions, the U.S. Central Intelligence Agency engineered a coup d'etat that led to the Shah's dismissal of Mossadegh as prime minister. Mossadegh launched a countercoup, and the Shah fled into exile. Taking advantage of the Tudeh party's bid to win power in then chaotic Iran, the reactionary monarchical elements of the army overthrew Mossadegh, whereupon the chief CIA agent in Iran, General Fazlollah Zahedi, became Prime Minister. The Shah returned from his brief exile and consolidated the Empire he would rule until his overthrow in 1979 by the Islamic Revolution.

The future of the NIOC was decided by an agreement reached with the Western oil companies. A consortium was formed consisting of American, British, French, and Dutch concerns to explore for new oil finds other than those to be found in Khuzestan. Additionally, the consortium would market all oil coming from Iran on a 50-50 profit-sharing basis with the National Iranian Oil Company. All oil, including that which was prospected in the new finds, had to be sold to the NIOC, which in turn would turn the crude over to the western consortium for marketing.

While the nationalization of Iranian oil and the formation of the Western consortium appeared to place Iran and the companies on an equal basis, this proved not to be the case. The amount of capital expenditure and risk involved in production is considerably more in the production stages of prospecting than in the latter stages of transportation and marketing, where the capital required is minimal. Therefore, the overall cost to Iran of producing the oil, the profit of which it would split with the consortium, was far more than that incurred by the consortium or its individual constituent companies.

The entire Iranian oil affair, while not directly involving the Arab states, proved to be a signal event in the subsequent history of Middle East oil. Further, it accelerated the point at which Arab oil would become the reservoir of Middle Eastern oil.

The Officer's Coup in Egypt, which ended the Egyptian monarchy in 1952, was the first republican nationalist action to be launched in the Arab world. The young military men who ascended to power, among whom was Gamal Abdul Nasser, began their tenure with an ideology that, in essence, demanded the ouster of foreign concerns that manipulated Egypt for their private interests. The pan-Arabism, state socialism, and anti-Israelism that Nasser would later preach came after the Sinai War in 1956. In reaction to Nasser's nationalization of the Suez Canal Company, British and French troops attacked Egypt with the cooperation of Israeli troops. Israel joined the European powers out of a desire to put an end to fedayeen (Arab guerilla) attacks emanating from Egyptian territory. Nasser's nationalization of the Suez Canal Company was, in turn, a response to Washington's refusal to provide increased aid to Egypt, particularly in the building of the Aswan High Dam. Following this series of rebuffs to his country, Nasser embarked on his anti-Westernism, a strain of ideology that would ignite the embers of disaffection latent throughout the Arab World, particularly in the oil-producing countries.

The events leading to and following the Suez Canal crisis were both nationalist and class in origin. Demonstrations in Jordan, for example, forced young King Hussein to reduce the overt power of his British advisors. In Saudi Arabia, the exploitative practices of Aramco were protested in a spontaneous demonstration by workers at the company's facilities in Dharan during a visit by the then reigning monarch, King Saud. Similar demonstrations had occurred just months earlier in Bahrain and Kuwait.

THE OIL COMPANIES' RESILIENCY IN THE
FORCE OF NATIONALIZATION

Expanding their policy of horizontal integration, the oil companies adopted a program to secure other oil concessions elsewhere in the Middle East to be prepared for any contingency. Exploration for oil was increased in Algeria and Libya, for example. The development of the north African reserves, though originally conceived as a contingency measure, uncovered a most productive find for the oil companies. Libyan oil, which is available in considerable amounts, is of a higher quality (lower in sulphur content) than other Middle Eastern oil. Further, it is closer to European and U.S. ports, and shipping costs were consequently reduced. The reduction in costs was not, however, followed by a reduction in price. The cartelization of oil by the companies preserved the arbitrary prices that had been agreed upon.

The rise of militant Arab nationalism, which was precipitated by Nasser's nationalization of the canal, was followed by nationalist outbreaks in Lebanon and Syria. The formation of the United Arab Republic in 1958, which united Egypt and Syria under Nasser, posed a threat to the pipelines that carried oil from Iraq and Arabia to the Mediterranean through Syria and Lebanon, a potentiality made even more threatening by the sabotage of the tapline at the time. The revolution in Iraq on July 14, 1958, which removed the Hashemite monarchy in that country and introduced the government of republic-oriented militarymen, prompted the United States and Britain to dispatch troops to Lebanon and Syria, partially to assist the ruling elites in those countries in their effort to suppress opposition elements, but more importantly to move against any threat to Iraqi oil installations. Following assurances from the government of Abdul Karim Kassem, the Iraqi dictator, that the oil facilities would be left unscathed by nationalization, there was a relaxation in the embattled posture of the Western governments.

The nationalization of the canal and other nationalist upheavals in the Arab core states was a watershed of an emerging awareness among Arab leaders concerning the power of their material and strategic resources. The Middle East had been transformed. Its leadership was no longer content with being the passive beneficiaries of royalties and revenues accruing from profits and decisions made by foreign interests. This, however, entailed a dilemma: the leadership realized that virtually their entire economic base was to be found in industries controlled by outsiders. The marketing of oil depended on foreign know-how, which had been assiduously retained by the Western oil companies. It was assumed that dispensing knowledge to native workers could result in a loss of control by the Western powers. Thus the wealth accruing from the oil resources was almost entirely contingent on the Western markets controlled by the oil companies. The extent to which the British, United States', and French companies could rely on the assistance of their governments in any contingency (as demonstrated by the deployment of Western troops throughout the Mediterranean, the Persian Gulf, and the presence of Western military bases throughout the region) illuminated the dependence of the Arab leadership on the oil companies. Despite this dependence, there were domestic forces operating in the Middle East that would no longer permit the exploitation of the region by foreign interests. The Arab leaders, particularly the feudal dynasts of the Persian Gulf region, were in search of a balance whereby they could retain the continued support of Western oil companies' governments, which were indispensable for the continuation of their misbegotten and antidemocratic rule, while placating domestic pressures for increased indigenous control.

The considerable scare that had been thrown into the oil companies and their governments by the nationalist activity of the late 1950s made them realize that the unabashed, unfettered extraction of petroleum resources could not continue as before. Nonetheless, there were economic interests to be preserved, even if the rate of their accrual and of their volume had to be slowed. As a result of contact with the companies and the emergence of an educated class of Arab technocrats, the Arab leadership had come of age, and they could no longer be treated paternalistically on the basis of an allowance or subsidy. Despite the fact that the new consciousness did not benefit or reflect the will of the citizens, the leaders of the nationalization movement comprised new power centers, or, rather, old power centers with evolved interests. Whether or not they represented the populace of their countries was inconsequential as far as the West was concerned; these indigenous elites had become the owners of the instruments of state power; and whether as the inheritors of feudal sheikdoms or as military dictators, they were the controlling powers in the Middle East. Those who held the reigns of state were the primary concern of the oil companies. The new consciousness manifested itself in the form of the Organization of Petroleum Exporting Countries (OPEC) and a new élan that flared in the various Arab capitals.

OWNERSHIP PARTICIPATION REPLACES PROFIT SHARING

There were several preludes to the emergence of OPEC, which affected the stability of conditions in which the oil cartel operated. The first of these involved the activities of smaller, independent oil companies (such as the Getty concern, and the Italian Ente Nazionale Idrocarburi [ENI]) that were attempting to undercut the cartel's monopoly by seeking concessions in areas where the majors did not operate (that is, the Saudi Arabia/Kuwait Neutral Zone) or in concession areas where friction had developed between the companies and the host country (as in Iran). The advantage held by the independents was their willingness to agree to a much smaller percentage of profits in exchange for the award of a concession from the host country. In other words, the size of the profits to be made in Middle East oil was so large that the independents could afford to share a larger percentage of the profits with the oil-producing countries. Although the overall effect of the entry of these independents into the industry did not result in extensive damage to the majors, it did indicate that the oil-producing countries might evolve a new attitude with regard to the majors. Eventually, the major companies realized that some concession in their mode of operation had to be secured if they were to prevent the erosion of their control over Middle Eastern oil resources. Gradually, therefore, they accepted a 50–50 profit-sharing formula with the oil-producing countries during the 1950s. The sheer magnitude of the profits to be gotten permitted the companies to suffer a cut in the percentage of their revenue.

The 50–50 participation formula did not, however, guarantee the type of parity between the companies and the countries that might be involved. In many cases, the profit-sharing formula applied only to production and not to revenues accruing in the much more lucrative transporting, refining, and marketing stages of the industry. Additionally, the companies frequently lowered the price of oil without prior consultation with the producing countries. Such reductions in prices were necessary to counteract the inroads made by the independent oil companies, which offered lower prices on the marketing end. The reduction in prices by the majors lowered the profit they made and, in some cases, reduced production. The oil companies were able to preserve their markets and their long-term profits. They were able to do so while concurrently reducing the manifest short-term profits, and therefore, reducing the amounts of profits that they were compelled to share with the countries.

One response to the pricing issue on the part of oil-producing countries was the nationalization in 1961 of 99 percent of the territory on which the Iraq Petroleum Company (IPC) had its facilities. This action by the Iraqi strongman, Kassem, was intended to quiet the clamor of Iraqi Communists and Nasserites for greater control by the government over its oil resources. While the IPC was able to continue functioning, the seizure of surrounding lands limited the exploration and production in which the company could engage. This was the first direct arrest of foreign control over oil facilities in a country governed by an Arab elite. However, it would not be followed by similar actions elsewhere in the Arab world until the early 1970s.

The more typical response to the pricing issue was adopted by Saudi Arabia and Iran, the two monarchical giants of the Middle East. This response entailed the notion of participation in ownership (as opposed to profit sharing) of production facilities as well as in decision making and management. This effectively changed the nature of Middle East oil from a "buyer's market," in which the oil-producing companies exercised control of Middle East oil pricing, to a "seller's market," in which the producers controlled the prices and production. In both cases the companies benefited; under the former arrangement, they represented both the buyers of oil and the sellers, since they acted unilaterally in controlling the price and rate of production and marketing. By entering into participation agreements with the oil-producing states, they remained the sellers; the countries would participate in determining the price of oil to the companies, but the companies would decide at what price to sell the oil to the Western markets.

The remarkable resiliency of the oil companies' price margins, despite the various changes in their control of Middle East oil, derives from their high degree of both vertical and horizontal integration. The companies have been able to weather profit sharing, participation formulas, and finally nationalization because they have secured involvement in all stages of the petroleum industry (production, transportation, refinement, and marketing), and they have been able to move from one production area to another. Nothing could or can cut into the profitability of the oil companies as long as the oil industry remains structured in its present form. The companies are able to determine their own prices, even though they no longer control production in the Middle East since the nationalization of oil facilities by the Middle Eastern states in the early 1970s. Although they have lost control in production, they are still able to preserve profits in the later stages of the industry and keep prices and profits at whatever levels they wish.

OPEC AS PARTNER, NOT AS ADVERSARY, IN THE OIL INDUSTRY

Despite the constancy in the status of the oil companies throughout the changes of Middle Eastern oil policies, there have been immense implications on the oil-producing states as a result of these changes. The formation of OPEC, in effect, formed a cartel of the oil producers that interlocked in partnership with the oil companies' own cartel. The oil-producing states determined the posted prices (the price of crude prior to the surcharges imposed by the companies in refining, transporting, and marketing), and they could regulate the availability of supplies (as evidenced, for example, by the "oil boy-cott" of 1973). However, they could not profit from their oil resources without the cooperation of the refining, transporting, and marketing arms of the industry, which have remained in the hands of the Western oil companies. This change in the control over Middle East oil does not, however, denote the loss of power on the part of the Western oil companies; rather, it results from a division of this control between the Western oil companies and the Arab ruling elites.

The power wielded by the Middle Eastern ruling elites permitted them to consolidate their control over their countries and to assume a pivotal role in world affairs, owing to the economic clout they pos-sess. The revolution that took place in the 1960s and 1970s did not involve a change in the structure of the Middle East oil policy, but rather allowed for the admission of the oil-producing states as part-ners in the enterprise, whose fruits the companies had previously been enjoying exclusively. As a result of this newfound partnership, the Arab and Iranian elites have been able to entrench their position in world affairs and have become the political pivots of the changed global economy brought about by the vastness of oil wealth. As the keepers of the world's oil, the Arab ruling elite have become sacro-sanct. The high degree of authoritarianism, the concentration of po-litical power in the hands of a royal family or clique, the denial of minority and other human rights and civil liberties, and the lack of democratic structures in the Arab world dovetails with the economics of Middle East oil. The power of the Arab bloc attests not to the legit-imacy of the individual regimes or the causes that they espouse but rather to their symbiotic relationship with the Western oil companies. Further, the oil-producing states have been able to use their petro-dollars to buy into enterprises in the West. Consequently, they have assumed a pivotal role in the global economic order.

Moreover, while it has been asserted that oil has become a po-litical weapon in the campaign to regain the territories captured by Israel in the 1967 war, there is ample evidence that the oil weapon is not employed to achieve political aims but rather is used to increase the economic power of the region's ruling elites. Naturally, the "boy-cott's" raising of petroleum prices also abetted the oil companies.

The present economic power of the ruling regimes in the Middle East is, as described above, the current manifestation of a process that extends to the period during which the Ottoman Empire entered its death throes. This process continued through the European pene-tration of the Ottoman Empire and included European colonialism and finally economic imperialism. This process continued with the involve-ment of Western oil companies in the region and has served as the key stimulant of the fantastic economic growth that the governments of the Middle East have enjoyed over the past two decades. These companies, and their governments, effectively serve as the accomplices of an increasingly entrenched system of government. The source of domination suffered by the peoples of the Middle East has merely shifted from foreign interlopers to native cliques. The persecution and violence that characterizes the Middle East today is no longer the product of foreign imperial machinations but of indigenous totalitarian elites. The latter's control over the region is bolstered by oil wealth, and their power has increased steadily without mandate from the citizens they purportedly represent.

5

UNREMITTING PASSION:
THE KURDISH NATIONAL MOVEMENT

On March 26, 1981, Serafettin Elci, who served as minister of public works in the government of the former Turkish Premier Bulent Ecevit, was sentenced by the Ankara martial law court to two years and three months in prison. The charge lodged against Elci by the military government that had ousted the Ecevit government in the autumn of 1980 was Elci's alleged creation of "propaganda with a view to destroying or weakening national feelings." The evidence of Elci's transgression consisted of statements he hade to the press while serving in the Ecevit government. The most incriminating of these statements was: "I am a Kurd. There are Kurds in Turkey."

Serafettin Elci is one of over 2,000 "secessionists" seized by the Turkish military junta following the coup of September 12, 1980. "Secessionists" is the code word used by both the military junta and previous Turkish governments in referring to Kurdish nationalists. The terms "terrorists" and "traitors" are additional code words used by Ankara to describe the 8.5 million Kurds that are estimated to live in Turkey and who comprise at least a quarter of that country's total population. Officially, the Kurds of Turkey do not exist; the Turkish government persists in referring to their country's Kurdish population as "Mountain Turks who have forgotten their mother tongue," a designation that first came into use during the Young Turks' reconstitution of the former Ottoman Empire after World War I. Anyone who today cites the Kurds when speaking of Turkey's "eastern question"—as Turkisk Kurdistan is euphemistically described by Turkey—risks arrest in that country. Indeed, an estimated 30,000 Kurdish detainees, comprising nearly half of Turkey's political prisoners, are now behind bars for "wrongdoings" pertaining to identification with the Kurdish national cause or for engaging in Kurdish communal activities.

The Kurds of Turkey are part of a nation consisting of 18 million people living on a historically and geographically contiguous swath of land that extends from eastern Anatolia through northeastern Iraq and Syria and deep into northern Iran. With the possible exception of the Berbers, the Kurds constitute the largest ethnonational group in the "Arab world." Often referred to as a "minority" group within Turkey, Iraq, Syria, and Iran, the Kurds are an overwhelming majority in that large expanse of land in northwestern Asia that had, until recently, been known throughout history as Kurdistan. Today, the Kurds are the second largest ethnicity in Iran; in Turkey and Iraq, they constitute the largest "minority" within these societies. In Syria, they follow the Druze and the Alawites on the scale of ethnic groups over which Damascus rules. Taken as a whole, the Kurdish nonstate nation is a formidable, albeit obscured force in the Middle East today. The suppression, discrimination, and persecution that the Kurds have faced over the past century is indicative not only of the subjugated status of this submerged nationality but of the general totalitarian system according to which Middle Eastern affairs are currently conducted.

Kurdistan is a large territory that is mountainous and generally inaccessible by conventional transport. The Kurds, according to tradition, are the descendants of the ancient Medes. They speak an Indo-European tongue similar to, but distinct from, Persian. They are neither Semites nor Persians, but an ethnically, linguistically, and culturally unique people. While the overwhelming majority of Kurds are Moslems, they include both Sunnis and Shiites. In Turkey, Iraq, and Syria, only 10 percent of the Kurdish population is Shiite. In Iran, however, 50 percent of Kurds are Shiites. Additionally, there are small numbers of Christian Kurds, Chaldeans, as well as a group practicing an offshoot of Zoroastrianism, the Yazidis.

As a predominantly Moslem community, the Kurds did not suffer any greater discrimination under the Ottomans than did other Islamic peoples. Kurdish was the vernacular among the Kurds, and tribal organization remained the traditional mainstay of Kurdish life under the Ottomans. Nonetheless, Turkish linguistic, cultural, and political hegemony affected the Kurds no less than it did the Arabs during the Ottoman realm. As with the Arabs, it was the demise of the Ottoman Empire in the late nineteenth and early twentieth centuries that awakened the Kurds to their national rights and collective aspirations. Unlike the Arabs, the Kurds did not attain independence or autonomy in the period since the fall of the Ottoman Empire. The struggle against their Arab overlords in Iraq and Syria and their Turkish and Persian rulers in Turkey and Iran has been the sine qua non of Kurdish national life through the past half century.

In addressing the Kurdish problem, one must speak simultaneously of the unitary and demographically homogeneous territory known

as Kurdistan, that is, of Kurdish society per se, as well as of the
Kurdish minorities in the various countries under whose jurisdiction
Kurdistan has fallen. Any discussion concerning the effect of the Kurd-
ish issue on contemporary Middle Eastern affairs—and the impact of
Middle East politics and economy on the Kurdish nation—must note
that the Kurdish national struggle still continues against the Iraqis,
Turks, Syrians, and Iranians with a great deal of viability and strength.
The eclipse of the Kurdish struggle from the view of the world does
not indicate any national debilitation on the part of the Kurds; rather,
the fact that the Kurdish problem is relatively unknown outside of the
Mideast represents the success of the governments ruling over the
Kurds in concealing the very existence of the issue.

THE KURDISH ISSUE AND THE EMERGENCE
OF MIDEAST POLITIES

The collective existence of the Kurds has been a problem for
all of the states in which the Kurds live. Three of these states—Turkey, Syria, and Iraq—are novel creations deriving from the various
settlements that concluded World War I. The histories of these countries as nations are short and replete with sectarian unrest and governmental suppression. These states, in order to survive, have mo-
bilized national legitimizing creeds, symbols, and superstructures
that project an image of national unity. This is true of Iran as well,
though it is less so than in the other states owing to the relative degree of independence that Iran enjoyed apart from the Ottoman Empire.
In order to enforce national unity in the states that now incorporate Kurdistan, the Kurdish national presence has been obfuscated
by the governing elites in the area. Both Iraq and Turkey have Kurdish
minorities entailing at least 25 percent of their populations. The Kurds
of Iran include at least 15 percent of that country's populace. The
Kurds of Syria, residing in the highly heterogeneous state that Syria
is today, are conspicuous not so much by their numbers but rather
by their identification with an ethnicity that includes large numbers
of people in neighboring countries.
Aside from their numerical weight, the Kurdish communities
of Iraq, Turkey, Syria, and Iran are vulnerable to governmental suppression for a number of other strategic reasons. Notable among these
reasons is economics and the intrinsic economic worth of Kurdistan
itself. An additional factor was the strategic value of the Kurdish areas
in the state-formation process and in reinforcing the ruling elites in
Iraq, Turkey, Iran, and Syria.
The Ottoman Empire incorporated all Kurdish regions east of
Persia. Consequently, the coup of 1908, led by the Committee for

Union and Progress, and the dissolution of the empire in the period after World War I were signal events in the emergence of the Kurdish national campaign. The establishment of states on the former Ottoman territories had a direct bearing on the Kurdish community, which included a considerable segment of the populations included in the incipient states.

The creation of modern Turkey by the Young Turks led by Mustafa Kemal Ataturk completely transformed the core of the former Ottoman Empire. The Young Turks were reform-minded, Western-oriented nationalists who foretold the death of the anachronistic Ottoman Empire. They were acutely aware of the misgovernment of Sultan Abdul-Hamid and that of his predecessors. They felt profoundly for the lingering feudal status of their Turkish people, and accordingly they believed that an end to the monarchy, with its governance of huge parts of Asia, Africa, and Europe and the populations residing there, was requisite. The Young Turks were also liberal capitalists who planned to build their new state, a republic, accordingly. Further, while they initially espoused a doctrine calling for the equality of all nationalities in the empire, the Young Turks proved to be chauvinists par excellence after assuming the reigns of government. The massacre of 1.5 million Armenians during the upheavals of 1915-16 and subsequent attrocities committed against the Kurds and Assyrians demonstrated the premium that the Young Turks placed on "equality."

But the Young Turks had a wearisome, almost herculean, task before them. The Ottoman system had left the Middle East depleted and chaotic. The Young Turks realized that the domains of Turkish sovereignty would have to be truncated, not only because of the terms of the postwar settlements, but also because of the unwieldy size of the former Ottoman domain. A new Turkey had to be rendered, one that would be cogent and responsive to the planning and government of a central authority. The hold maintained by the clerics on the minds of the masses that had allowed the sultan/caliph, veiled by a religious mystique, to misgovern the realm had to be abolished. Consequently, the Young Turks proved to be ruthless in the secularization of the emergent Turkish state. A new Turkish identity was conceptualized—and enforced—by the Young Turks. This identity admitted no sectarian differences, no linguistic variety, no government involvement in the affairs of religion, and vice versa; it would tolerate no acknowledgment of any subnational allegiances or any other identity that could lead to potential cleavages in the nascent nation. Consequently, the Armenians, Kurds, Assyrians, and all other communities residing in the borders were "turkified" in every way possible.

THE RISE OF KURDISH NATIONALISM

Parallel to the emergence and coming to power of the Young Turks was a similar process among Kurdish intellectuals. Similar to the al-Faht and al-Fahd organizations that developed among Arab intellectuals and military men, expatriate Kurdish nationalists formed the first Kurdish grouping transcendent of tribal boundaries. The Khoybun, which came about on the eve of World War I, was based on an ideology composed of ideas propagated in the turn-of-the-century periodical titled Kurdistan. The Khoybun was able to realize only a few of its aims, due to the lack of national and social consciousness among their people and the tremendous political currents sweeping imperial Europe and the Middle East. Nonetheless, the Khoybun marked the coming to age of the Kurds as a people in struggle against the forces of external domination.

According to the terms of the Treaty of Sevres, which, was convened, in part, to dispose of the former Ottoman domains, an independent Armenian state and an autonomous Kurdish region were to be established. This was in accord with the "Fourteen Points" advocated by President Woodrow Wilson and his doctrine of national self-determination. Although it provided for Armenian and Kurdish self-determination only within a fraction of Ottoman Armenia and Kurdistan, the Treaty of Sevres was accepted by the Armenian and Kurdish representatives, who realized that international recognition of their sovereignty over slivers of their land was better than no recognition at all. After all, the distribution of the former Ottoman lands was carried out first and foremost to cohere with the interests of the Entente powers. Of course, it would be even better if this could be done in a way that achieved self-determination for the besieged national communities. The Kurds did not delude themselves when they accepted an autonomous, albeit truncated, Kurdistan. Imperial interests were the determining factor in the achievement of their autonomy, just as they had been in the awarding of Arab independence in the Hejaz, Transjordan, Iraq, and Syria.

The Treaty of Sevres, for all its shortcomings, provided some measure of international recognition of Kurdish and Armenian national rights. The Treaty of Sevres, however, never achieved fruition and was superseded by the Treaty of Lausanne (1923). The latter was meant to resolve the Turkish War of Independence (1919-23), in which the Young Turks attempted to oust the Greek, British, and French troops that occupied their country. In this attempt, Mustafa Ataturk sought to assure the Moslem population of his country that the War of Independence was being waged in order to rid the country of the "infidel" invaders, and that all Moslems of the Ottoman nation—Turks and Kurds—would share equally in the upbuilding of the incipient state.

The Kurds of eastern Anatolia at first cooperated with the revolutionaries, given the impending absorption of their territory into what appeared to be an encroaching Soviet-backed Armenia. The Turks were loathe to lose any more land than was necessary to placate the imperialists, and certainly no land would be ceded to the "infidel" Armenians or Greeks. Consequently, the Great National Assembly of Turkey was convened in autumn 1920, and three years of Turkish military struggle led by Ataturk against the Armenians, Georgians, and Greeks took place with the cooperation of the Kurds of Turkey.

Gradually, it became apparent that the Turks had no intention of sharing power with the Kurds. In fact, they supressed Kurdish nationalist groupings as early as 1919 and declared by 1922 that their goal was a "Turkish" state. By the time that the Treaty of Lausanne was signed in 1923, the Turanian character of the state was consecrated into international law. No mention of a free Armenia (the short-lived Armenian republic [1918-20] had already been absorbed by the Soviet Union) or of a Kurdistan was made. The imperial powers recognized the authority of Ataturk's Turkish government, and an inflow of Western capital into Turkey was a result of the treaty. This cohered with the liberal bourgeois vision adhered to by the Young Turks, and it was with this financial assistance that the Young Turks were able to construct their Turkish republic.

THE KURDS OF TURKEY

Following the proclamation of the Turkish republic, the Kurds of Turkey rose in revolt against President Kemal Ataturk in March 1924 under the leadership of Sheik Said of Palu. Ataturk's ruthless efforts to "turkify" all national minorities in his country (particularly the Kurds) resulted in the rapid spread of Kurdish rebellion throughout the east and south of Turkey. The Turks employed tens of thousands of troops under an air umbrella and surrounded the rebels in April 1924. By the thirtieth of June 1924, Sheik Said and 46 of his followers were executed by the Turks. It is estimated that 80,000 Turkish troops converged on the general area, destroying 206 Kurdish villages and massacring 15,200 individuals.

As a result of Sheik Said's revolt, the Turkish government imposed sanctions suppressing the use of the Kurdish language, forbidding the establishment of Kurdish mosques, and placing restrictions on Kurdish dress. These sanctions further inflamed nationalism in Turkish Kurdistan. In 1927 the Khoybun assisted in the insurrection organized in the areas north and east of Mt. Ararat. The fighting continued for three years until the Turks crushed the Kurdish rebellion. In 1930, another uprising flared up, led by Kurds who had served as officers in the Turkish army. The Turkish infantry, backed by the air force, decimated the uprising in less than a month.

The Turkish premier during the late 1920s, Ismet Inonu, was dedicated to the complete destruction of Kurdish nationalism. His government received considerable assistance in their activities against the Kurds from the Persians, who had also been suffering from Kurdish insurgency in their country. The wounds incurred by the ill-fated resistance in Turkish Kurdistan left the Kurds sapped of energy and unable to continue their fighting. The Khoybun, which had been largely associated with the various revolts in Turkish Kurdistan, was discredited in the eyes of their people as a result of the severe punishment they suffered at the hands of the Turks.

Lacking leadership, and crippled by its unsuccessful attempts at achieving national minority rights; the Kurds of Turkey fell to the superior Turkish military forces. Beginning in the middle of 1937, the Turkish government sent troops into the mountains of Kurdistan in order to bring the Kurds fully under their cultural as well as political and economic control. However, stiff resistance was encountered by the Turkish troops. A four-month rebellion aimed at setting up an independent Kurdistan on Turkish territory was launched by the Kurdish minority. The Turkish Kurds were assisted in this endeavor by Kurds in Syria, and Soviet-supplied weaponry and support made the insurrection even more potent, despite the fact that the Soviets were also arming the Turks.

After considerable fighting, the Turkish military finally succeeded in putting down the rebellion by imposing a hermetic martial rule over the eastern sectors of the country. After being disarmed, the Kurds were detribalized and their traditional leadership was eliminated. All outward forms of Kurdish identity were suppressed, and the Kurds assumed the status of virtual indentured servants in Turkish civil projects. As far as the Turkish government was concerned, Turkey no longer had a Kurdish community in its populace; Kurds had become "Mountain Turks who have forgotten their mother tongue."

Although the Kurds resisted their collective subjugation vigorously and violently, they have remained a suppressed, submerged subnational group in Turkey until today. In a country known for its economic hardship, illiteracy, and lack of social services, Kurdistan in Turkey is the most underdeveloped region of both the Turkish republic and of Kurdistan as a whole. No meaningful industrialization has taken place in the area, and its rich farmlands are utilized for such cash crops as tobacco, which is extracted from the Kurdish areas to benefit the Turks. Over the last decade, a clandestine Kurdish resistance movement has been operating in eastern Turkey, assisting Kurdish insurgents in Iraqi and Iranian Kurdistan and providing the rudiments for a Kurdish renewal in eastern Turkey. With the termination of civilian rule following the military coup of September 1980, the Turkish military government, whose raison d'être was the elimination of the fragmentary fighting between the political left and right in the country, clamped down severely on Kurdish activists in particular and Kurdistan in general. Evidently, considerably more Kurdish activity was undertaken in eastern Turkey under the civilian governments than had been previously acknowledged, and much of what passed as fighting between politically polarized Turks was, essentially, the activity of the Kurdish resistance. Since the coup, large amounts of the Turkish military have reportedly been posted in the country's eastern region in an attempt to crush any nascent Kurdish insurgency.

In the post-World War I period, the value of Kurdistan to the Young Turks was considerable. The latter were dedicated to retaining as much land under Turkish sovereignty as possible, and the usurpation of the Kurdish regions was part of a single process in the turkification of the new republic—a process that began even prior to statehood with the Armenian Massacre. Moreover, it was feared that any concessions to Kurdish national sentiment once the Turkish republic was created posed dire dangers to the national unity that the Young Turks sought to forge. Despite the fact that the denial of Kurdish self-determination ran counter to international law as stipulated in the Treaty of Sevres, the European imperialists recognized the potency of the Young Turks Revolution as evinced by the Turkish prowess during the War of Independence. Consequently, the imperial powers capitalized on the sordid situation by recognizing the organizing of the Turkish republic along the lines demanded by the Turkish nationalists. The recognition of a bourgeois, Western-oriented regime in Ankara afforded the Europeans an entrée to Eastern markets and resources in a country where the leadership was positively predisposed toward them. In the case of Turkish Kurdistan, and, for that matter, Armenia, economics and power triumphed over proclamations of adherence to the principle of self-determination.

THE KURDS OF IRAQ

An even more graphic example of the sacrifice and manipulation of the Kurdish cause for the benefit of foreign imperial interests and those of native elites can be found in the case of Iraqi Kurdistan. While the Turks were more proficient at suppressing Kurdish identity and communal affiliation, the Iraqis devoted their energies to brutally crushing Kurdish nationalism. Iraqi Kurdistan had been an integral part of the Kurdish nonstate nation as the Ottoman vilayet of Mosul. Traditional Kurdish feudal structures functioned in Mosul with little interference other than the ubiquitous demands for increasing taxation emanating from the Sublime Porte.

The situation in Iraqi Kurdistan changed with the enhanced co-operation of the Ottomans and the Germans. The latter were awarded the concession for the building of the Berlin-to-Baghdad railroad in return for their assistance in buttressing the Ottoman regime. The German Anatolian Railroad Company had received rights to exploit whatever minerals were to be found along the route taken by the Berlin-Baghdad railway. Concurrently, the militarization of the German society produced demands for enhanced military capacity, particularly the improvement of naval capability. This enhancement was found in the utilization of oil as a fuel that would increase the efficiency and speed of German warships. As a result, when German engineers detected oil deposits in the Mosul vilayet, the Berlin-Baghdad railway was detoured through the region solely in order to extract the oil that was to be found there.

With the defeat of the Axis powers in World War I, the question of Mosul arose. Oil had become an increasingly important commodity for the Entente powers as well, considering the utilization of motorized air, sea, and land transport. The British especially realized the importance of Mosul oil, and they acted to gain control of the former vilayet by incorporating the region into the nascent Iraqi state. However, Mosul had been allocated to the "French Zone" of the Middle East under the terms of the Sykes-Picot Agreement of 1915, which had allocated the lands of the tottering Ottoman Empire in advance of its dismantlement. The French agreed to cede Mosul to the British in 1919, after the latter provided the French with a block of shares amounting to 25 percent ownership of the British-dominated Turkish Petroleum Company (later the Iraq Oil Company).

Additional complications developed in the British plans to integrate Mosul into the new kingdom of Iraq when the Turkish republic challenged British rights to the territory. As a former vilayet of the Ottoman realm, the Turks argued that Mosul should logically be included in the reconstituted republic of Turkey. The entire fiasco figured highly in the resolution of the Turkish War of Independence, and no negotiated settlement could be attained between the British and the Turks. Consequently, the League of Nations placed the entire question before the International Court of Justice at the Hague. The latter ruled that the question of Mosul was an internal Iraqi affair over which they had no jurisdiction, and this decision was effectively a vindication of the British position. As a result, Mosul was grafted onto the Iraqi state, which was then composed of two disparate former vilayets, Baghdad and Basra.

The interesting part of the disposal of the Mosul question was the totally cavalier way in which the people of this oil-rich territory had their fates decided for them without their consultation. With the British decision to join Mosul to the Arab Hashemite Kingdom of Iraq, the Kurds who had conducted their own affairs on their ancestral lands for millennia became a subnational group in an Arab state. As with their Turkish kin, the Kurds of Mesopotamia became pawns of imperial economic interests and subjects of a foreign culture, language, and regime whose interests bore no resemblance to their own.

Initially, Kurds participated in Iraqi public life. With time, however, it became apparent that Iraqi interests were in fact Arab interests, and there was no evidence of any desire among the Arab clique that controlled the country to share power with the Kurdish minority, which accounted for at least a quarter of the population and was a majority in the country's northeastern regions. Recognizing that Iraq was ruled by a self-interested Arab elite, the Iraqi Kurds began to build activist organizations with the aim of maximizing their interests in Iraqi Kurdistan and, if possible, winning autonomy or independence.

Initially, well-educated Kurdish leaders were placed by the British in key positions within the native bureaucracy in an attempt to coopt the Kurdish population into the fabric of Iraqi society. Among these Kurdish officials, the British appointed Sheik Mahmoud Barzanji as the governor of the Suleimaniya district of Iraq. A Kurdish nationalist, Barzanji allied himself with Iranian and Turkish Kurdish tribes in a revolt aimed at winning a free Kurdish state. With the careful deployment of the Arab Iraqi army, the British put down the Kurdish revolt in the summer of 1923. Barzanji, owing to his heightened stature within the Kurdish community as a result of his leadership in the revolt, was reappointed governor of Suleimaniya by the British just a few months after the rebellion. In less than a year, Barzanji attempted but again failed to take Suleimaniya as the capital of an incipient Kurdish state. The indefatigable Barzanji and his followers retreated to the mountain fastness of Iraqi Kurdistan and attempted their enterprise once more in 1926. Finally dislodged by the Iraqi army in 1927, Barzanji was subjugated for a time by the British-puppet Iraqi regime.

Political efforts to achieve national minority rights were also undertaken by the Kurds in Iraq. In 1928 the Kurdish members of the Iraqi Chamber of Deputies petitioned the government in order to attain some measure of autonomy in Iraqi Kurdistan. When the Iraqi government failed to respond to the petition, the Kurds called a successful but inconsequential boycott of the 1929 elections. With the Kurdish nationalist fervor running high, Sheik Barzanji escaped house arrest and fled to Iran, which was in an anarchistic state of affairs and could offer no resistance to Barzanji's declaration of a free Kurdish state in the Kurdish wilds of the country. Barzanji launched an invasion of Iraq in an effort to join both Iranian and Iraqi Kurdistan together. Barzanji was eventually captured by the Iranians, who cooperated with the Iraqis in shattering the Kurdish movement and extradited Barzanji to Iraq.

After a few years of relative calm in Iraqi Kurdistan, the British attempted to settle Assyrians in the Barzan region of Iraqi Kurdistan. The Assyrians were refugees from persecution in Turkey, and their resettlement was viewed by the British as a humanitarian imperative. The Kurds viewed the resettlement scheme as a British attempt to intervene in Kurdish affairs as an attempt to dilute Kurdish society. A revolt led by Sheik Ahmed of the Barzani tribe was proclaimed and proved to be a watershed of simmering Kurdish disaffection with their status as second-class citizens in the contrived Iraqi state. The initial revolt by Sheik Ahmed failed; however, the Barzanis became the undisputed leaders of the Kurdish national movement in Iraq to the present. The famed Kurdish leader Mullah Mustafa Barzani, brother of Sheik Ahmed and the father of Idrifs and Ubeidullah Barzani, the present leaders of the Kurdish revolt in Iraq, was until his death in 1979 the recognized military and political leader of the entire Kurdish nation.

Some abatement in the plight of the Kurds living under Iraqi rule took place with the coup in 1936 that brought General Bakr Sidki, a Kurd who had nothing at all to do with organized Kurdish affairs, to power as premier of Iraq. Though an assassin's bullet ended Sidki's term after only a few months in office, the premier distinguished himself for little else other than his supervision of the massacre of some 18,000 Assyrians in 1932. Therefore, the extent of his loyalty to the Kurdish national cause remains unknown even after his death.

The Iraqi and Iranian Kurdish national movements were fermented during World War II after the British moved into Iraq in order to oust the pro-Axis Premier Rashid Ali Gailani. In Iran, the Soviets and the British jointly occupied the northern and southern zones of the country after German agitation among Iranian nationalists was exposed. Iraq and Iran were crucial strategic objectives as far as the Allies were concerned, and consequently the administration of the countries could no longer be entrusted to the power centers that the Western imperialists had installed when the Iraqi state was created. As a result of the loss of native (that is, Arab and Persian) control over Iraq and Iran, and given the Allies preoccupation with waging war against the Axis powers, the Kurdish nationalists busily set out to establish enduring nationalist organizations.

Among the first attempts made at such organization was the establishment of the Komula i Zhian i Kurdistan in September 1942. The Komula, as it later became known, was created by Kurdish intellectuals under the tutelage of the Soviet Union. The Komula was modeled after communist-style political cells that operated in a clandestine fashion. Based in Mehabad in Iranian Kurdistan, the Komula was able to muster sufficient Kurdish military might to oust the Iranians from the Mehabad area in May 1943. During subsequent years, Mehabad became a major center for Kurdish national activity.

A host of Kurdish nationalist organizations began to proliferate The Khoybun enjoyed a modest revival, particularly in the towns and villages. Those Kurds who had not yet been detribalized or urbanized were suspicious of both the Khoybun, due to its association with the ill-fated Kurdish revolts in Turkey, and the Soviet-backed Komula. Another group, the Heva (lit. "the Hope"), sprang into existence, having elicited the support of Kurdish intellectuals on both sides of the highly permeable Iraqi/Iranian border running through Kurdistan. The sole objective of the Heva was the creation of an independent Kurdistan. Another party, the Kurdish Nationalist Party (KNP) consisted primarily of Iraqi Kurds, but it had many Iranian and Turkish Kurds as members. The stronghold of the KNP was the oil-rich areas of Iraqi-Kurdistan around Kirkuk, Mosul city, Suleimaniya, and Abril. KNP chapters also existed in Baghdad, where the Heva also maintained a strong presence and had its headquarters. Unlike the KNP, however, the Heva was leftist in political orientation and had an articulated ideology that was presented in its periodical Azadi (Freedom). The leftist strain of Kurdish nationalism was reinforced by the large presence of nationalist Kurds in the rank and file and the leadership of the Iraqi Communist Party (ICP), which at times has functioned almost as if it were a Kurdish nationalist organization.

THE BARZANIS

The dominant Kurdish movement, however, had at its center the Barzanis, with Mullah Mustafa at the helm. Held under house arrest from 1932 to 1943 as a result of his brother's leadership of the Kurdish Revolt during the Assyrian incident, Barzani escaped from Suleimaniya into Iran and incognito into Iraq where he fortified alliances with various Kurdish communal leaders on both sides of the border. The Barzani-led forces (to be known from then on as the peshmergas, lit. "those who face death") engaged in a number of attacks against Iraqi installations in retaliation for Baghdad's violation of agreements that had been reached with the Kurds. Concurrently, a Turkish Kurdish leader, Sheik Said Biroki, led peshmergas in attacks against Turkish facilities. For some time, there existed a transnational Kurdish insurrection struggling in concert in Iraq, Iran, and Turkey. The Turks were successful in obliterating the peshmergas fighting on their side of the border, and this put an end to Kurdish nationalist activity until the past decade.

The Iraqis, however, were confronted by a seemingly invincible Kurdish resistance. The acrimony between the Iraqi Arabs and Kurds intensified with time. A few cosmetic changes were made by the Iraqi regime, such as the appointment of a token Kurd to the Iraqi cabinet.

The Kurds became increasingly frustrated and by the summer of 1944 they launched a spontaneous, intense, though poorly organized revolt against the Iraqi government. Recognizing the need for unified action and greater strength, the Kurds of Iraq and Iran began to organize a transnational political movement. The Iranian branch of the Komula produced a flag for the all-Kurdistan liberation movement. Representatives of the Turkish, Iranian, and Iraqi Kurds met for a first all-Kurdish conference at the foot of Mt. Dalanpur (Iran), where the frontiers of all three countries meet. The long-term goal agreed to by those in attendance at the conference was the establishment of an independent Kurdish state, geographically congruent with the demographic presence of the ethnic Kurds in the Middle East.

Despite the creation of an umbrella organization, the ideological Kurdish parties often found themselves at tactical cross-purposes. Given the similar leftist orientation of both the Komula and the Heva, it would have made political sense for the two parties to enter into political alignment or merger, but neither party was willing to become a subordinate to the other.

In the short run, the Heva became the loser for its refusal to merge into the Soviet-backed Komula. Many prominent sheiks, including Qazi Mohammed, a charismatic political and religious leader of the Persian Kurds of Mahabad, joined the Komula. Qazi Mohammed became the recognized, though unofficial, leader of the Komula, and thus the Komula became an acceptable alternative for the grassroots Kurdish masses.

In Iraq, the ICP splintered into the Kurdish Communist Party (which, despite its Kurdish composition and support for the Kurdish national movement, included many non-Kurds among its members) and the ICP. Even though the Komula was Soviet-backed, there was never any real cooperation between the three communist-oriented groups in Iraq during the war. A united front, the Rizgan i Kurd (Kurdish Deliverance), was formed by the groups, although the front was contrived. The three groups, as well as the Heva maintained a heavy though ineffective correspondence with the Allied powers in the hope of winning Allied support for their particular programs of Kurdish nationalism. Each party contacted the Allies independently, though none received the support they sought.

The Barzani cadre, which was politically unaffiliated (although it exploited the Heva, which was cooperative in the anticipation that Barzani would become its leader and thus add strength to the organization), received some initial response from the Allied powers. Barzani's fighting success made him the subject of limited scrutiny as a possible alternative native power center that might represent Western economic and political interests better, perhaps, than the existing Arab centers. Delegations of British diplomats met with Barzani's emissaries, but little came of these meetings. The British continued to support the Arab elite in Baghdad.

It became apparent that Barzani was considered the leader of the all-Kurdish national movement, both by the Kurdish leadership and the masses. In February 1945, Barzani had formed the Freedom Party, which served to organize his followers and consolidate his position at the helm of the Kurdish national movement. Barzani's group received recognition as the dominant element of the Kurdish movement, and it emerged as a sophisticated and politically cunning organization, whose military might was unrivaled by any other Kurdish force.

During March 1945, in acknowledgment of Barzani's obvious stature as the leader of the Kurdish minority in Iraq, Iraqi Premier Nuri Said made the nearly fatal mistake of granting Barzani amnesty for his actions taken during the British occupation. Barzani's power grew rapidly, particularly after he increased his bold guerrilla activities. Throughout the spring and summer of 1945, the Barzani-led peshmergas had the Iraqi military on the run and completely routed the Iraqi army and police facilities. An attempt to disarm Barzani in August of 1945 resulted in heightened confrontation between the Kurdish and Arab Iraqis.

Realizing the potential threat posed by the Barzani revolt, the Iraqi government sent large contingents of troops to put down the rebellion. Iraqi brigades, well armed and backed by armor as well as artillery, were humiliated at the hands of the Kurdish partisans, who adopted a hit-and-run strategy that could not be controlled by the Iraqi ground troops. The Iraqi air force was called in to prevent the loss of further ground by the infantry. War planes bombed villages, trapping the Kurdish fighters and civilians while Turkey closed its borders to the refugees.

During September 1945, the Iraqis were able to restore some degree of control to the situation by exploiting Kurdish intertribal rivalry and utilizing Turkish collusion to ensnarl the Kurds into a tight net. In early October Barzani still refused to surrender. Realistically appraising his military predicament, however, Barzani fled Iraq with a contingent of 9,000 people, including no more than 3,000 armed men. Under the cover of darkness, the Barzani loyalists entered Iranian Kurdistan. Arriving at Kurdish-held Mahabad district, the Barzani partisans enjoyed some relief from the relentless fighting and maneuver. It was made clear from the beginning that Mahabad was under the control of Qazi Mohammad's Komula. Finally, it seemed that the Barzanis were subservient to another Kurdish group. The Komula, it appeared, had the war-weary Barzanis under its control.

THE KURDISH PEOPLE'S REPUBLIC

The Persian Komula groups had been easily enticed at the conclusion of World War II by Soviet promises of financial assistance and
supplies of material. Qazi Mohammed and his aides visited the Soviet
Union just before Barzani brought his fighters and families to Mahabad.
The Soviets, at that time, promised the Komula its help in securing
Kurdish autonomy. The understanding was that independent Kurdistan
would owe its allegiance to the Soviets.

At the same time, in the northern sector of Iran, the Soviets
were giving similar aid to the Azerbaijanis, another Iranian national
minority group. Within one month, northern Iran had been cleansed
of any Iranian governmental presence and was in the process of Sovietization. On December 12, 1945, the Democratic Party of Azerbaijan was formed by the Azerbaijani nationalist groups with the objective
of independence. Less than a month later, the National Government
of Azerbaijan proclaimed an independent Azerbaijani state.

While the Democratic Party of Azerbaijan was formed, Qazi
Mohammad announced that the Komula was transforming itself into
the Democratic Party of Kurdistan (DPK). The DPK was avowedly
nationalistic, with demands for the uninhibited use of the Kurdish language, the self-rule of Kurds in Kurdish areas, the distribution of
Kurdish wealth exclusively in Kurdish areas, and the creation of a
Kurdish council. Prima facie, the DPK was aiming toward autonomy
within the Iranian state framework. The analogies, however, between
its development and that of the Democratic Party of Azerbaijan, were
too strong to be ignored: obviously the Soviet's strategy was the creation of a free Kurdistan just as a free Azerbaijan had been established.
Due to national hostilities, however, there was no cooperation between
the Sovietized Azerbaijan nation and the Soviet-backed DPK. The DPK
and the Freedom Party, while clearly overlapping in many realms,
remained separate parties due to Barzani's fierce determination to
be subordinated to no one.

Soviet arms began to arrive at Mahabad throughout the late fall
and early winter of 1945. A printing press was brought and the Kurdish newspaper, Kurdistan, was revived. Symbols of Kurdish self-
determination were widely evident, from the flying of the Kurdish flag
to the use of the traditional Kurdish manner of dress. An infrastructure had been formed and on January 22, 1946 Qazi Mohammad declared the independence of the Kurdish People's Republic. Mohammad
proclaimed himself the country's first president and a cabinet was
assembled.

The recently deposed Shah of Iran, Mohammed Reza Pahlavi
had taken over as the monarch of his country in 1941. His desire to
overrun the Kurdish republic was repeatedly stated, though he was

prevented from doing so by the threat of Soviet intervention on the be-half of Qazi Mohammad. His efforts were consequently limited to propagandizing against the Kurdish republic and limiting the latter's sovereignty to an area extending to no more than 50 miles in radius.

The Soviets proposed the merger and full incorporation of Azer-baijan and Kurdistan into the Union of Soviet Socialist Republics. The rivalries between the two peoples, rather, between their two govern-ments, mitigated against such a merger. In addition, Britain's with-drawal from Iran in accordance with the schedule of the Tripartite Agreement, which was signed at the end of the war, forced the Soviets to grudgingly withdraw their troops from occupied Iran. The Soviets promised that they would supply the Kurds with armaments, including heavy artillery, transport, and armor, after their withdrawal from Iran's northern occupation zone. Five thousand pistols and rifles and limited Soviet training was all that Moscow did in fact provide to the Kurdish forces, which were led, primarily, by the Barzanis. Although a military hierarchy was developed, including experienced Kurdish former Iraqi and Iranian army officers, the Kurdish military presence lacked the necessary major military equipment.

Squabbling between Azerbaijan and Kurdistan did little to pre-pare the two fragile countries for the Iranian forces massing on the southern Kurdish border after the Soviets withdrew on May 9, 1946. Since mid-April, the Iranians had attempted to move into Kurdistan. However, the forces on the front line, mainly Barzanis led by Mullah Mustafa, successfully repulsed them. This successful resistance gave added prestige to the Barzanis. An overconfident Kurdish High Com-mand even entertained notions of launching an offensive of their own in order to incorporate all of Iranian Kurdistan.

By late May, the Barzanis had made a few costly tactical errors in the field, and internecine fighting between urbanized and tribalized Kurdish units took place. Inner dissension and military setbacks forced the Kurds to enter into prolonged negotiations with the Iranian com-manders. Barzani, despite heavy losses, made up for the setbacks by undertaking to defend the entire southern front with Iran through the exclusive use of his own loyalists. Meanwhile, adventurist Kurdish forces in the north, toying with the idea of launching an offensive, were forced to withdraw from their positions on the Azerbaijan border.

The Soviets, with an eye on Iranian oil, strongly urged the Kurds to abandon their goal of retrieving more of Persian Kurdistan. The Iranian oil fields were becoming increasingly tempting to the Soviets, who wanted to control the oil flow through political rather than mili-tary means. By August 1946 Qazi Mohammad was in Tehran in search of amnesty, if not for a more honorable settlement. The Persian gov-ernment, though, was determined to de-Sovietize the northern Iranian regions. By December 13, 1946, the Azerbaijan republic collapsed as

Iranian troops marched, with relative ease, into its capital, Tabriz. Two days earlier, sensing impending doom, Barzani had moved his forces to the Iraqi frontier. On December 16, 1946, Qazi Mohammad surrendered and the Kurdish People's Republic fell to Iranian control. Qazi Mohammad and three other Kurdish leaders were hung.

After the fall of Mahabad, Barzani tucked his troops deep into the mountains and went to Tehran to negotiate a settlement with the Iranians, who were not anxious to risk an imbroglio with Barzani's partisans. Various proposals were made by the Iranians, all of them requiring Barzani's disarmament, but the other Barzani leader, Sheik Ahmed, refused the Iranian offer. Consequently, negotiations were broken off between the Barzanis and the Iranians.

Determined to dislodge the Barzanis, the Iranians commenced an offensive, including strafing by air, to push the Barzanis out of Iran or into compliance. Enraged by Iranian ruthlessness, Mullah Mustafa Barzani was committed to fighting the Shah's troops. His followers, however, resolved to discontinue the fighting and returned to Iraq. As a result, various leaders of the Barzanis were hung, and Sheik Ahmed surrendered to endure detention, once again, at the hands of the Iraqis. Mullah Mustafa, along with several hundred dedicated followers, fled across the border to the Soviet Union, where he remained in exile for 11 years, through 1958. The Iraqis began a concerted campaign of persecution against the Kurds on their territory, not distinguishing between Kurds who had been involved in the fighting and those who had not.

Little Kurdish political activity took place during the period in which Barzani was exiled. The only respite granted the Kurds was in Iraq where, due to frequent coups and cabinet reshufflings, the Kurds were able to take advantage of governmental weakness.

FRAGMENTATION AND REUNIFICATION

In 1954 the Kurdish Democratic Party (KDP) became the United Democratic Party of Kurdistan (UDPK). The party was Marxist-Leninist in ideology, but foremost it was a Kurdish liberation movement. Its branches took root in various Iraqi cities, and it was operated almost identically to the Soviet Communist Party. Communists dominated its politburo and Mullah Mustafa (who could hardly be called a socialist, less so a Marxist-Leninist) was appointed in absentia leader of the UDPK. The party, being nationalist in outlook, was determined to capitalize on Barzani's name while he was in exile since he could not offer any dissent.

In 1958, as a result of a republican-oriented military coup for which the Kurds of Iraq and particularly the UDPK took credit, several

Kurds were placed in government positions. Premier Abdul Kassem placed several members of the UDPK, along with Baathists, in his cabinet. An amnesty was granted to those who had been a part of the Kurdish revolts, including Sheik Ahmed. But at all times, Kassem vigorously reminded the citizens that they were Iraqis first and only secondly Arabs or Kurds. This reminder was directed at the Kurds since Iraqi governmental power was firmly held by the Arabs. The provisional constitution, while denying the request from the UDPK that autonomy be granted to the Kurds, stated that: "Arabs and Kurds were considered partners in the homeland . . . their national rights within Iraqi sovereignty are recognized."

Kassem agreed with the UDPK that Barzani was the true leader of the Kurds and, after hesitating for a few months, he agreed to let Barzani return from exile. Desirous of establishing strong ties with the tribal Kurds, Kassem demanded that Barzani accept the presidency of the UDPK's politburo. The acceptance of the UDPK's leadership was the sole condition attached to Barzani's amnesty. Anticipating that Barzani had become suitably Sovietized, the UDPK sent a delegation to the Soviet Union to escort Barzani back to Iraq. They quickly learned that Barzani would not have his nationalism linked to any sectarian trend. Barzani was kept under moderate house arrest, when he brazenly announced, upon his return to Baghdad, that he would not forgive the Iraqis for crimes committed against the Kurdish people during the latter's postwar insurrection.

During 1958 and 1959, Kurdish requests for such benign privileges as the publication of a Kurdish newspaper and the celebration of the Kurdish new year festival were increasingly refused, despite the participation of the UDPK in the government. At the same time, Barzani was commanded to order his forces to defend territory under Kassem's rule from Iraqi counterrevolutionaries. Kassem had established the Popular Resistance Force (PRF), which was, in effect, a private, socialist militia in defense of his regime. The presence of the Barzanis among the Popular Resistance Force patrols of Iraqi Kurdistan incurred the ire of the tribalized mountain Kurds. Finally, Kassem, the UDPK, and Barzani realized that the Kurdish rural masses were not responsive to the accelerated rate with which the "Revolution" was being forced on them. The political arrests and the allocations of land reforms met with strong opposition, particularly from those Kurds who had received Barzani properties after Mullah Mustafa and his followers had been forced into exile a decade earlier.

The Iraqi Communist Party (ICP) led by Kurds who were sympathetic to Kurdish civil demands (though not to national minority rights), formed a Covenant of Cooperation with the UDPK. The party, though basically communist in the composition of its membership, agreed with the ICP on most matters, except the issue of Kurdish autonomy.

As the Nasserite elements began to grow in Iraq, a coup was attempted by Iraqi pan-Arabists in 1959. Barzani and the UDPK, along with the ICP, supported the status quo ante; that is, they supported Kassem. The Kurds knew that Kassem was the closest they would come to a sympathetic Iraqi leader, and hence Barzani stood by Kassem's Free Officer's Regime.

Kassem, after repeated anti-Kurdish revolts erupted throughout Iraq during 1959, proscribed the activities of the ICP and the PRF on the grounds that they had attempted to usurp his power by eroding his authority and by inciting the Arab population against the Kurdish minority and against his political allies. Additionally, it was rumored that the ICP and the PRF had conspired to have Mullah Mustafa Barzani assassinated. Kassem began to suspect his own Free Officers Movement of antigovernment aspirations. He dissolved the movement and moved closer to Barzani. The UDPK, at Barzani's insistence, withdrew from its pact with the ICP. As a reward, Kassem permitted the publication of a Kurdish periodical, Khabat. The UDPK was purged of anyone who had been involved in the forging of ties with the ICP, and in an effort to alter its image the party changed its name to the Democratic Party of Kurdistan (DPK). Along with membership in the DPK came the right to bear arms, a privilege denied to Kurds who were not DPK members.

THE FIVE IRAQI WARS AGAINST THE KURDS

During May 1960, the Fifth Kurdish Congress was held. The DPK, primarily due to Barzani's stature, prevailed as the stewards of the congress, and Barzani was elected chairman of the DPK. Barzani's hope that a transnational Kurdish congress would be achieved was prevented by the repression of Kurds in Iran, Turkey, the Soviet Union, and Syria.

While the Fifth Kurdish Congress was being held, Kassem, concerned that Barzani was emerging as too strong a force in Kurdistan, entertained the leaders of Kurdish tribes who were hostile to the Barzanis. While Barzani was fully accepted as the foremost spokesman for the Kurds across Kurdish party lines, partisan friction between members of various parties remained. Kassem sought to consolidate his control over Iraq at all costs, since Iran and Iraq were involved in a conflict impinging on Kurdish national rights, namely, the conflict of claims over the Shatt-al-Arab river basin.

The clampdown by Kassem on the UDPK, including arrests of numerous officials and the forcing of the organization to go underground marked the growing deterioration between Kassem and the Kurds. The DPK, considered to be the dominant representative of the detribalized Kurds, was perceived as a Soviet interloper in an era when Kassem was becoming progressively anti-Communist. It was true that many Kurdish politicians, Barzani excluded, were Communist sympathizers. Barzani and Kurdish nationalism, however, were virtually synonymous. Despite his untainted nationalism, Barzani used the typical technique of powerless nations, namely, playing one power against the other. Visiting the Soviet Union in November 1960 on the pretense of attending the October Revolution celebrations, Barzani attempted to persuade the Soviets to strong-arm Iraq into providing the Kurdish national minority with communal rights. Barzani's effort to move the Soviets toward the assistance of the Kurds met with utter failure. The Soviet's apathy to the plight of the Kurds hardened Barzani. His call for allies unheeded, Barzani realized that the Kurds would accomplish their aims only by their own travail.

Kassem's paranoia over Barzani's popularity explains why Barzani was permitted to go to the Soviet Union in the first place. During the Kurdish leader's absence, Kassem incited those few Kurdish tribes who were opposed to the Barzanis to attack his organization and his followers. On the pretense that this intertribal, political infighting was wreaking chaos and bringing the country to anarchy, Kassem took several repressive steps against the Kurdish community. These measures included the closing down of the Kurdish newspaper, the cancellation of a Kurdish teacher's conference and the promotion of Arab anti-Kurdish sentiment. As a result, Barzani's life was imperiled and he was forced to travel with an armed entourage.

The intertribal rivalry, while partially directed toward the Barzanis, was really a protest against the domination of the DPK in representing the Kurdish community. Barzani's association with the DPK, despite the fact that Barzani considered this a marriage of convenience, prompted much of the anti-DPK Kurdish hostility to be aimed at him. Withdrawing from Baghdad, Barzani returned to Barzan where he could carry out his Kurdish national activism unfettered by political exploitation and betrayal. The DPK continued to function in Baghdad and still maintained that Barzani was their leader, again exploiting his name and stature.

The Kurds put forth increasingly strong demands to Kassem, including requests that revenues from oil extracted in Kurdistan be shared on an even basis between the Kurds and the Arabs. The Arabs' anti-Kurdism increased and tensions rose. One of Barzani's sons was arrested in Baghdad and the only contact remaining between the government and Barzani was Sheik Ahmed, whom Kassem considered to be a friend due to his lack of support for the continuance of Kurdish nationalism.

From March through September 1961, the Barzanis consolidated their forces in the mountains, knowing that a major imbroglio between the government and the Kurds was imminent. The struggle between the Kurds and the Iraqi Arabs continued throughout the 1960s and was largely unnoticed by the rest of the world, despite its intensity and the genocidal character of the Iraqi offensives against the Kurds. The Iraqi air force regularly napalmed, bombed, and strafed Kurdish villages. The Kurds were forced to coalesce into a guerrilla organization despite pitifully inadequate supplies. World War I-vintage rifles and pistols were the weapons used by the Kurds against the latest Iraqi imports of modern heavy armor, artillery, and aircraft. Barzani was both commander-in-chief of the Kurdish forces and the political leader of the Kurds, and he received the loyalty of the overwhelming majority of Kurds of all classes and sectors. During 1961 and 1962, Barzani's fighting force swelled in number. While the Kurds in Turkish, Soviet, Syrian, and Persian Kurdistan were held in place by an iron fist, the Iraqi Kurds fought virtually alone throughout the 1960s.

The study of the 1960s revolt and the subsequent 1974-77 rebellion is basically the study of the politics of betrayal. The Kurds continued to seek and receive assistance from whomever they could, a tactic that served as a survival technique but was detrimental in the long run. The Barzanis, while maintaining a relentless guerrilla war against the Iraqis, would often find themselves assisted by one government, only to find at a later time that the same government, now back in grace with the Iraqis, would turn their backs on the Kurds.

The 1960s rebellion consisted basically of four Iraqi offensives. The first of these began with Kassem's dissolution of the DPK and the flight of the Central Committee of the DPK to territory held by Barzani. Therefore, all Kurdish forces loyal to Kurdish national rights were concentrated in the mountains. Government military actions against the Kurds in December of 1961 were met by a counteroffensive by the Barzanis. The details of these and subsequent actions represent an immensely fascinating study of how a poorly equipped, yet tremendously devoted and well-disciplined, Kurdish guerrilla force could hold the powerful Iraqis indefinitely at bay.

The Barzanis were not the only fighting Kurds in the mountains. The DPK developed its own peshmergas, which emerged as an astoundingly effective fighting force. Kurdish irregulars also joined the nationalist fighters in the Kurdish Revolt, although the Barzani peshmergas were regarded as the official standing army of the Kurdish nation.

Intimidated by the almost magical fighting qualities of the peshmergas, Kassem offered the Kurds complete amnesty in return for the laying down of arms and allegiance to Iraqi central governmental authority. Barzani, riding high on the wave of success, refused the amnesty offer. In fact, in the late spring and early summer of 1962, Barzani launched an offensive against the Iraqis, bolting down from the mountains to harass them in apparent disregard of the fact that the Iraqi troops were numerically larger and much better equipped. The Iraqis moved an entire infantry division to Mosul in July 1962. In their desperate effort to put down the Kurds, Iraqi aircraft recklessly bombed Turkish settlements that they had mistaken for Kurdish villages. Therefore, hostilities, though limited in scope, ensued between Iraq and Turkey.

In 1963 another Free Officer's Coup, similar to the one that had placed Kassem in power and that was influenced by the Baath, overthrew Kassem. As a result, a group known as the Committee for the Defense of the Kurdish People's Rights was formed at Lausanne, Switzerland by Kurdish exiles, who called for Kurdish independence throughout Greater Kurdistan. The committee devoted itself to fund raising and the acquisition of a respectable image. It issued statements disavowing any connection between the Kurdish liberation struggle and communism. Within Iraq, negotiations were undertaken between the government and the Kurds under the leadership of Barzani and the DPK. As a result, a ceasefire was arranged.

In the meantime, the Soviets found it politically expedient to befriend the Iraqi Kurds, since Barzani was obviously a power to be contended with as the leader of a Kurdish minority that existed in the CENTO countries. Through the offices of the Mongolian People's Republic, the Soviets put the question of Iraqi genocide against the Kurds before the United Nations General Assembly in May 1963. Suddenly, with no apparent explanation, the Soviets had the Mongolian delegation withdraw the matter from the General Assembly's agenda. Subsequently, no United Nations discussion on the Kurdish question has ever taken place.

From June through September 1963, a second full-blown Iraqi offensive against the Kurds was initiated. The coming to power of a Baath regime in Syria and the merger of the Syrian and Iraqi High Commands produced the placement of a Syrian brigade at the disposal of the Iraqis for use against the Kurds. The Kurds began to develop a program of urban sabotage, including the demolition of oil pipelines and bombings in and around Iraqi major cities such as Baghdad. The Syrian air force joined in an offensive along with Iraqi aircraft, and the Iraqis steadily gained ground. By August 1963, while the Kurds and the Iraqis were supposedly in negotiations, areas deep within Kurdistan were overrun by Iraqi troops. In the same month, the existence of a transit and supply line between Turkish and Iranian Kurdistan to the Iraqi Kurds was uncovered, and the Turkish and Iranian governments began to assist the Iraqi-Syrian High Command in crushing the Kurdish uprising by breaking its supply lines. The number of troops and the superior Iraqi-Syrian firepower increased, yet the Kurds were successful in making territorial inroads and retook some of its land lost in earlier battles.

By November 1963, the Baathists were fighting among themselves concerning, inter alia, the domination of the Syrians or Iraqis in the control of the Joint Iraqi-Syrian High Command. In Iraq, street fighting broke out, a coup successfully brought down the Free Officers regime, and a new government was formed. By February 1964, a ceasefire between the Kurds and the new Iraqi regime was announced and the new pro-Nasser government of Taher Yahya was installed. By May 1964, a new provisional constitution was adopted, proclaiming that the Kurds would have "nation rights within the Iraq national unity." At Barzani's insistence, the constitution was amended to state that the Kurdish people's ". . . development would be parallel with the Arabs in Iraq."

The Kurdish communists in the DPK were opposed to the ceasefire, and friction ensued between the communists and the noncommunists in the DPK. Barzani was satisfied with the ceasefire, which he understood to be only a tentative step pending the satisfaction of Kurdish demands during subsequent negotiations with the new government.

Yahya's regime permitted the existence of only one party, the pro-Nasser Arab Socialist Union. The ICP and DPK were thus proscribed. The DPK had made contact with the Shah after the futility of seeking support from Nasser had been made clear to them. The Shah, apprehensive about a strong central government in Baghdad that might threaten his status in the Persian Gulf region, began to encourage the Iraqi Kurds, though he did not provide them with material assistance. The DPK continued its armed struggle without the active participation of the Barzanis. The Barzanis enjoyed the confidence of the rural Kurdish masses, who were alienated from the DPK due to the presence of the radical elements within that organization. The masses supported Barzani in his effort to drive the radicals out of the DPK and into Iran. In Iran, the Shah announced that he would provide refuge to the purged DPK members so long as they disarmed and did not agitate among the Iranian Kurds. The exiled DPK refused these conditions for refuge and attempted to reenter Iraq with the help of some Persian Kurds. The Barzanis prevented their admission back into Iraq.

In July 1964, Barzani won support as the unrivaled leader of the newly purged DPK, and he proceeded to convene a new DPK Congress at which time the organization was reconstituted. The DPK radicals continued to receive the support of certain exiled Kurdish intellectuals, but the grass-roots of the Kurdish nation, particularly in Iraq, gave Barzani a mandate to direct the national movement as he saw fit. By September 1964, Barzani agreed to allow some of the exiled radical DPK leadership to return to Iraqi Kurdistan and rejoin the DPK as long as they remained entirely subordinate to him. Many of the purged DPK members returned to assist in the incipient struggle that was to emerge as the Third Iraqi offensive against the Kurds.

In October 1964, Barzani accused the Iraqi Government of pursuing a policy of forced "Arabization" similar to the "Turkification" imposed on the Kurds in Turkey. He cited continued repression of the Kurdish community in Iraq, including forced migrations of civilians. Rapidly becoming disillusioned with the promises that the government had made during the signing of the ceasefire and noting Nasser's continued apathy toward the Kurdish question, Barzani convened an all-Kurdish Congress in early October. It was resolved that the DPK and the other Kurdish factions would coalesce in order to create a Kurdish governmental and civil infrastructure. A Kurdish legislature was elected, as was the Military Council of the Revolutionary Command and the Executive Committee. Financial institutions were created and, in less than a month, three-quarters of Iraqi Kurdistan was under the tight control of the Kurds led by Barzani.

Kurdish frustrations over the government's delaying tactics resulted in greater Kurdish militancy. A new coalition, including the ICP and the Baathists, was formed in Iraq and seemed close to real power. The coalition called for the creation of a "Nasserite democracy." Barzani had learned from previous experience that the Baathists could not be trusted and the DPK refused to join the Nasserites. In January 1965, Barzani, fearful of another Iraqi onslaught, radically reduced the Kurds' demands for national minority rights put forth to the government in Iraq.

In early spring 1965, the Iraqi head of state, Yahya, was dispatched to Cairo to apprise Nasser of the impending offensive against the Kurds. Nasser adamantly disapproved of the planned offensive, not out of pro-Kurdish sympathies but because he did not want any fissures or diversions in the Arab campaign against Israel, a campaign that Nasser, at the time, was attempting to solidify. Despite Nasser's disapproval, the Iraqis ordered an armored column into Kurdistan in early April, followed shortly thereafter by nine brigades composed of 40,000 troops. The Iraqis pushed forward under an air umbrella provided by its fighter planes, and the Kurds, as in the last two offensives, were forced further into the mountains. Napalm, strafing, and mortar bombardment were utilized; defoliation was also employed, and the Kurds resorted to what was, by then, well-practiced guerrilla tactics and sabotage techniques. The Kurds, deeply embedded in the mountains, prepared to repel the oncoming Iraqi assault against them. In July 1964, the government initiated a program for the harassment of Kurdish civilians, including indiscriminate arrests, dispossessions of land, and massacres.

The Iranians, again betraying the Kurds, cooperated with the Iraqi military in a series of joint campaigns. Apparently fearful that Kurdish nationalism would contaminate Iranian Kurds, the Shah attempted, without success, to close his border to any supply and communication lines that existed between Iraqi and Iranian Kurds. The Turks placed mines in a wide swath of its common territory with Iraq in order to prevent Kurdish infiltration from, or retreat to, Turkey. Given consistent Kurdish resistance and an uprising by the Yazdi national minority group in the west, the Iraqis discontinued their offensive against the Kurds. While there were still some antinationalist Kurdish tribes that the government used to harass the Kurds' resistance, larger Kurdish tribes defected from the government's fold and joined the nationalist movement. In the long run, the Iraqis lost more than they had gained by launching the offensive. Additionally, the DPK and the exiled radicals were almost entirely reconciled. The radicals returned to Iraq and assumed their old positions in the DPK. Barzani, disgruntled with the superpowers, claimed that both the United States and the Soviet Union had refused to provide the Kurds with armaments and supplies during the revolt, thus reneging on previous commitments. Allegations that the Iraqis had employed nerve gas against Kurdish civilians were also made by Barzani.

In September 1965, another Iraqi government was installed under the premiership of a supposedly moderate civilian, Abdul Rahman al-Bazzaz. The Kurds took a wait-and-see attitude concerning the new regime. Time showed that Bazzaz was even more anti-Kurdish than his predecessors. Bazzaz viewed Kurdish nationalism as a divisive force working against the economic and political progress of Iraq. At the same time, the Kurdish Revolt served to preserve the military in positions of power on the pretext that military preparedness had to be maintained in order to ward off the Kurdish threat. Bazzaz turned to President Nasser, whose obsession with building an invincible, indivisible anti-Israel Arab bloc was growing in intensity. Nasser, on October 22, 1966, openly declared his support for the Iraqi regime's plans to completely eliminate the Kurdish problem.

The Kurds had faced three wars in less than half a decade, and their restlessness and rage were growing. The peshmergas consolidated their position in Kurdistan, particularly in the mountains, and a great deal of supplies traffic went between Iraqi and Iranian Kurdistan. The Shah had a covert role in maintaining the Kurds, who were confronted with a fourth Iraqi offensive in January 1966. The Iran/Iraq hostilities were growing in pitch, and the Shah was interested in subverting the successful restructuring of Iraqi society.

The Iraqis adopted an attitude of "no negotiations or amnesty with the Kurdish rebels." Ostensibly, taking military actions in the mountains of Kurdistan in the middle of winter would seem suicidal, since the Kurds had so much familiarity with the mountainous region. Two brigades and a large detachment of Special Forces Commandos made some initial inroads against the peshmergas during the opening days of the fourth offensive. The peshmergas quickly repulsed the

Iraqi advance line with considerable casualties being sustained by the Iraqis. Barzani, frightened at the Iraqi commitment to Kurdish destruction, sent an urgent memorandum to the United Nations, seeking a commission of special inquiry into Iraqi atrocities against Kurdish civilians. His pleas for U.N. intervention were disregarded.

Further desperation was added to the Kurdish situation in that the exiled radicals, to whom Barzani had granted amnesty, were attempting to double-cross him with the assistance of the Iraqi regime.

The Iraqi government's campaign against the Kurds of 1966 was embarrassingly unsuccessful. Despite heavy concentrations of firepower against the severely ill-equipped Kurdish forces, the Iraqis were frustrated in their attempts to exorcise the peshmergas. On June 29, 1966,Bazzaz was forced to present to the Kurds a peace proposal, which included far-reaching concessions toward self-determination within the Iraqi state. Barzani immediately accepted the peace proposal, although they fell short of declaring complete Kurdish independence or even autonomy.

The DPK radicals, while having negotiated the actual peace settlement with the Iraqis—the settlement was viewed as a virtual Iraqi surrender—did not gain the prestige they had sought. Barzani emerged as the triumphant hero.

During the winter of 1967, after a few more Iraqi regimes had come and gone, the Arab effort against Israel preoccupied the Iraqi government to the neglect of the implementation of the Kurdish rights program. The pounding received by the Arabs during the 1967 Arab-Israel War, including the psychological and limited military casualty received by Iraq, resulted in the creation of yet another Iraqi government. Elements within the DPK, including the incorrigible head of the radicals, Talbani, attempted to usurp Barzani's power. Talbani accused the Barzanis of cowardice in not reacting forcibly enough to the nonimplementation by the government of the 12-point peace program. Talbani and his clique went so far as to join the government-sponsored Saladin Force (sabotage squad), which, among other objectives, was used indirectly against the Kurds.

In 1968 sporadic incidents of Kurdish strikes at government installations continued. On July 12, 1968, the government fell once more, and the new government lasted only five days, when General Hassan al-Bakr assumed power in a Baathist military coup. Though his government pledged to implement the 12-point program, in actuality he supported the Talbani group in its attempts to wrest control of the DPK from Barzani. In October 1968, the government sent troops to assist the small Talbani faction against the Barzanis. Barzani contacted the United Nations with accusations that the Iraqis, with the cooperation of Kurdish turncoats, were practicing genocide. No material relief came from any agency of the United Nations.

In January 1969, the Iraqi government launched a short-lived offensive against the Kurds. Barzani retaliated with a successful counteroffensive in early March. In April of that year, an unsuccessful attempt to destroy the Kurdish nationalists was made by the Talbani group, who raised a force of approximately 1,000 mercenaries with the support of General Bakr.

Fortunately for the Kurds, hostilities between Iraq and Iran were intensifying over rival land and water claims to the Shaat-al-Arab river. The Shah, in order to continue the destabilization of Iraq internally, provided critical supplies to the peshmergas. While receiving arms from the Soviet Union, the Iraqi government began to enter into negotiations with the Kurds. In the midst of the negotiations, the government launched another attack against the Kurds in September 1969, in the hope of eliminating one source of Iranian intrigue in Iraq. The peshmergas completely destroyed the Iraqi offensive.

The Iranian/Iraqi situation grew steadily worse and, while no Iranian troops fought alongside the Kurds, there was an open flow of Iranian and Iraqi Kurds between the two countries. The status quo persisted through 1969 with the Kurds not being dislodged or compromised. Finally, Bakr made overtures to Barzani for a peaceful solution, which Barzani insisted would have to be sanctioned and enforced by the United Nations. In January 1970, after surviving an Iranian and U.S. Central Intelligence Agency-backed coup, General Bakr's government reaffirmed the 12-point program for Kurdish national minority rights that had been previously adopted in 1968 as the basis for a rapprochement with the Kurds. The settlement, finally signed by the Iraqi minister of the interior and two of Barzani's sons on March 11, 1970, allowed for complete amnesty for Kurdish POWs and political prisoners. The 15-point program incorporated the original 12-point program and was intended, in Bakr's words, to be "a permanent solution that will last forever" and would grant genuine autonomy to the Kurds. By the end of 1970, many of the points of the armistice agreement between Iraqi Arabs and Kurds had been arrived at, although the shared revenues of the Mosul oil wells and the issue of a Kurdish vice-president in Iraq were not resolved. Nevertheless, it appeared by all accounts that the peshmergas had finally reaped some of the fruits of their struggle.

THE IRAQI-IRANIAN COLLUSION AGAINST THE KURDS

The situation in Iraq was such that, until 1974, the status quo of March 1970 prevailed. The Kurdish leaders took al-Bakr at his word, and it was anticipated that, through negotiations, the Iraqis would honor the pledges he made in the 1970 15-point program. Throughout the period, Bakr's standing army included more than 90,000 troops, which were supported and trained by the Soviets. The Iraqi arsenal included 1,200 tanks and over 200 fighter jets, while the Kurdish arsenal consisted basically of small arms, some of which dated back to Ottoman days, and artillery and armor of only the most rudimentary stock.

By March 1974, it had become apparent to the Kurds that the Iraqis had no intentions of fulfilling their part of the bargain. Hostilities recommenced in March 1974, and during the succeeding twelve months it is estimated that the peshmergas lost approximately 600 fighters, while the Iraqis are said to have lost nearly 60,000 troops. Iraqi airborne attacks resulted in tens of thousands of Kurdish civilian casualties. Militarily, the 1975-77 Iraqi offensive was so askewed in terms of armaments that one Kurdish cannon often struggled against more than 300 Arab tanks; the Kurds had no antitank weapons. Much of the urbanized population, even professionals and academics among the Kurds, when hearing of the new offensive, left their homes and went to the mountains forming an all-Kurdish peoples' auxiliary, including a network of schools and hospitals.

For the Kurds, the financial hardship of the anti-Iraqi revolt had been extreme. For the Kurdish refugees fleeing persecution in non-Kurdish Iraqi cities, camps had been created in Iran under the auspices of Iran's Red Lion and Sun society. Until 1975, the Iranians assisted in the financial upkeep of the revolt, and additional sums were received from "other sources." It is widely assumed that Israel assisted the Kurds in a variety of capacities throughout their revolts against the Iraqi regimes. The extent and specifics of this assistance has not been made public. While the fighting persisted, the Kurds also managed to continue cash crop farming, the most lucrative crop being tobacco.

Despite an extensive network of checkpoints on all roads leading out of Iraqi Kurdistan, the Iraqi troops were unsuccessful in interrupting the flow of supplies, both military and relief in nature, that flowed from Iran to Iraqi Kurdistan. The Kurds had become so effective at smuggling that they were able, for the first time in the history of their national liberation movement, to bring Iranian-supplied artillery, anti-aircraft guns, and other heavy armaments across the Iranian/Iraqi frontier.

When the Kurdish military offensives had assumed awesome successes against the Iraqis, Iran's Shah increased his assistance to the peshmergas. The Shah hoped that by keeping the Iraqis busy with the Kurdish imbroglio, he would preserve his hegemony in the Persian Gulf region. The Iraqis, recognizing the Shah's intent, deported the bulk of Iranians then living in Iraq, most of whom were Kurds, arrested many of them, and hung several of their leaders. The Kurds were, therefore, benefiting from the increase in the mutual preoccupation between the Iraqis and Iranians.

Nearly 15,000 Iraqi troops that were massed against the Kurds were killed or wounded during their campaign to roust the <u>peshmergas</u> from their mountain hideouts. The Kurds were the indisputable victors in their struggle to force the Iraqis to honor the 15-point program for Kurdish autonomy. The Kurdish dream for autonomy, however, was crushed by an unexpected rapprochement between their Iranian patrons and the Iraqis. Again the Kurds had been betrayed.

At a meeting of the Organization of Petroleum Exporting Countries (OPEC) held in Algiers on March 6, 1975, Shah Mohammed Pahlavi and Sadaam Husain Tikriti, then vice-president of Iraq, signed a peace pact. For their part, the Iranians would receive substantial concessions, including the virtual domination of the mouth to the Shaat-al-Arab river on the Persian Gulf. The Iraqis, in return, found a face-saving device from their humiliating defeat at the hands of the Kurds in the withdrawal of all Iranian support. Even passive use of Iranian territories as supply routes and for refugee camps was to be denied to the Kurds. In the single month following the signing of the Algiers pact, 90,000 Kurdish refugees, fearing for their lives at the hands of the enraged Iraqis, crossed into Iran. These Kurds were restricted to camps and received no assistance at all from the Iranian regime. The Turkish government boasted that 150,000 Kurds attempted to enter into its territory but were turned back lest they incite the "Mountain Turks" into revolt.

As part of his willingness to grant "amnesty" to the refugees, the Shah called for immediate Kurdish disarmament. Barzani, hunted by the Iraqis, fled into Iran. There he was briefly detained before continuing on to the United States where he remained in exile. After a long battle with cancer, Mullah Mustafa Barzani, the greatest Kurdish leader of the century, died in early March 1979 in Washington, D.C., where he spent his last years in exile. His death, as his liberation struggle, was barely noted by the media.

THE IRANIAN KURDS: TREACHERY IN TEHRAN

In reviewing the history of the Kurdish revolts during the 1960s and mid-1970s, one finds that Iran's interests in giving aid to the Kurds were purely self-serving and treacherous. The Shah's sole interest in supporting the Kurds was to use them as pawns in his up-and-down relations with Iraq. When he achieved what he had sought from the Iraqis, the Shah betrayed the Kurds without the least bit of compunction. While the pact between Iraq and Iran would seem to leave Iraqi troops, previously committed to combatting the Kurds, open for deployment on the Iranian border, Iran knew it could rely on Iraq's adventurist designs on the rest of the Middle East to occupy its soldiers. The Iraqi Baathists were still trying to subjugate the Syrians, and Iraq still had claims to Kuwait. The Shah also knew that the Iraqi generals could be kept busy with pan-Arab plots to destroy Israel. The Shah, therefore, had not jeopardized his strategic interests by withdrawing his support for the Kurds.

The latent Kurdish uprising—the first since the betrayal of the Kurds in 1975—began almost simultaneously with the coming to power in 1979 of the Khomeini-Bazargan regime in Iran. Iranian Kurds participated wholeheartedly in the Iranian Revolution to depose the Shah but, in the words of Ayatollah Ezzedin Hosseini, one of the leaders of Iran's Kurds:

> We fought in the revolution not out of religious convictions but for political goals. We want autonomy—our own Parliament, our own language, our own culture. The revolution has destroyed despotism, but it has not ended the discrimination against minorities.*

The tensions between the Kurds and the Iranians were exacerbated by the fact that the majority of Iranians are Shiites, while most Kurds are Sunnis (although 50 percent of Iranian Kurds are Shiites). The tensions finally erupted into violent demonstrations within days of Mehdi Bazargan's advent to power. The first demonstrations broke out, appropriately enough, in Mahabad, the site of the short-lived Kurdish People's Republic. The result of the uprising was 23 fatalities and 40 Kurdish fighters and government troops injured. Cognizant of the Kurdish adage "Kurdistan or death," Khomeini quickly invited Ayatollah Hosseini to Tehran for "discussions." The Kurdish leader declined an offer to enter into negotiations because of the subordination of the Kurds that Khomeini intimated would have to form the basis of negotiations. Additionally, Khomeini had not indicated any willingness to recognize the Kurds as anything other than Iranians who happened to include a large number of Sunnis among them.

The Kurds' defiance of the Ayatollah Khomeini's status as the ruler of Iran made the Islamic regime anxious to nip any incipient Kurdish rebellion in the bud. Consequently, Khomeini dispatched Iranian Minister of Labor Daryoush Farouhar to negotiate with Hosseini in the mountains of Kurdistan. Forouhar walked away with no concessions from the Kurds; he was presented with an eight-point program that the Kurds demanded be implemented if they were to desist from their threatened revolt.

---

*The New York Times, March 1, 1979, p. A3.

A violent struggle broke out between Khomeini loyalists and the Kurds within weeks of the labor minister's visit to Kurdistan. In a coup de main, the Kurds in the city of Sanadaj expelled the Revolutionary Council loyal to Khomeini and installed a council of their own choosing. The area around Sanandaj was saturated with Kurdish villagers who fought in hand-to-hand combat to wrest control of the city's army garrison from the Khomeini forces. The fighting that began on March 17, 1979 was so intense and fearsome that Ayatollah Khomeini sent them his closest aide, Ayatollah Mahmoud Teleghani, religious leader of Iran's Shiites, to negotiate with the Kurds. Joining Ayatollah Teleghani was Minister of the Interior Seyyed Sadr-Haj Seyyed Javadi, Flexing his muscle, Khomeini also sent the highest ranking military official of the Bazargan government, chief of Staff General Vali Ulla Gharani, to demonstrate the government's resolve in putting down the rebellion, either through Kurdish acquiescence or by military force.

The four days of fighting in Sanandaj saw poorly armed Kurdish irregulars battling Iranian troops and armor. One hundred Iranian soldiers perished and reinforcements had to be called into action.

On March 24, 1979, the Iranian government and the Kurdish leadership announced that a formula had been arranged that would bring a ceasefire into effect. A joint committee of Iranians and Kurds would govern Sanandaj for a month until elections could be held to install a Kurdish district government. The Kurdish villagers, at Hosseini's request, honored the ceasefire and returned to their homes. Hosseini was confident that his followers' show of strength would frighten the Iranians into compliance with the terms of the ceasefire.

On April 4, 1979, it became clear that the Revolutionary Government was following the tradition of perfidy that the Kurds had been confronted with in the past. Former Prime Minister Mehdi Bazargan announced that all promises made to the Kurds would be considered null and void. The Kurds, according to Bazargan, would submit to the authority of his government or be crushed. The tensions continued with constant Kurdish guerrilla raids conducted in defiance of Bazargan's ultimatum.

In order to avoid a clash between the fragile Iranian military forces and the potent Kurdish peshmergas, Ayatollah Khomeini again dispatched his closest aides to negotiate a settlement with the Kurdish leaders. During the spring and summer of 1979, the highest ranking Iranian military, political, and religious leaders were sent to Kurdistan and met with both Sheik Hosseini and the political and military leader of the Kurdish Democratic Party of Iran, Professor A. R. Ghassemlou, who had returned to Kurdistan from Czechoslovakia where he had been exiled during the 1960s and 1970s. By mid-summer, it had become apparent that little compromise was being produced by the negotiations, and the Kurdish parties announced the formation of a "Congress of Oppressed Peoples in Iran" aimed at consolidating the Kurdish, Azerbaijani, Turcoman, and Baluchi national minority movements against the domination of the Shiite Iranianism promoted by the Islamic government. The creation of such a front was an anathema to the Iranian regime, and by late summer 1979 a full-scale war between government troops and Kurdish peshmergas and Azerbaijani militia ensued.

The fighting between the minorities and the government spread and created unrest among the Turcomans and the Baluch, as well as among the Kurdish and Azerbaijani masses. Consequently, the government deployed a large part of its military forces in the Kurdish and Azerbaijani provinces. The Iranian forces, having encountered stiff resistance from the peshmergas, were ruthless in their assaults, and as a result of their superior firepower and troop strength, they routed the Kurdish irregulars handily.

In late 1979 and throughout 1980, the Kurdish peshmergas in Iran took advantage of the state of war with Iran and launched a new insurrection. As the Iraq-Iran war dragged on, the Iraqi government was said to provide support of an unspecified nature to the Kurdish insurgents in Iraq. This assistance took place, ironically, against the increased activity of the Iraqi Kurdish nationalists, who denounced the regime of Saddam Hussein as being fascist and reactionary. The Iraqi Kurdish Democratic Party under the direction of two of Mullah Mustaf Barzani's sons, Ubeidullah and Idris, started peshmergas operations against the Iraqi government. Presently, as both Iraqi and Iranian Kurds engage in insurgency against their respective rulers, the degree of cooperation between the Iraqi and Iranian Kurdish nationalist forces is uncertain.

SYRIAN KURDISTAN

Currently, the Kurds continue to endure their status as a non-state nation. This situation persists in the face of ongoing inattention to, and neglect of, their plight by the world community. Kurdish resistance movements function with varying strength in the major Kurdish centers of Turkey, Iraq, and Iran. In all three of these countries, the imposition of national unity policies by the central government continues the suppression of the Kurdish communities located there. Turkey has attempted to "turkify" its Kurds. Iran continues to view its Kurdish population as a troublesome rural population who, though speaking a different language, are entirely Iranian. The Iraqis have been so threatened by the activities of the Kurdish inhabitants of oil-rich Mosul that they have attempted assaults of genocidal dimensions against the insurgents. Syria has incorporated a portion of Kurdistan

in its Jazerieh district, which borders Turkey. Beginning in the late
1950s, with the coming to power of the pan-Arab Nasserist regime in
Damascus, the Syrian Kurds, who number under half a million, formed
a Kurdish Democratic Party modeled after the Kurdish Democratic
Party (KDP) in Iraq. Although certain tensions had previously existed,
the creation of the Syrian KDP was more a sign of a nationalist renaissance than of any meaningful resistance against Arab oppression.

In the early 1960s, petroleum deposits were found in the midst
of Syrian Kurdistan. Additionally, the Nasserists had been replaced
by the even more pan-Arabist Baath Party, and the persecution of the
Syrian Kurdish community gathered a terrible momentum. The Kurds
had been accused of having smuggled into the Jazerieh region hundreds
of thousands of Turkish Kurds for the purpose of diluting the "Arab"
character of the region. A 12-point official government program was
devised that sought not only to "Arabize" the Jazerieh region through
the imposition of Arab language and culture and the resettlement of
Arab peasants in the region, but also sought to subject Syrian Kurds
to: dispossession of their lands; restrictions on professional, educational, and social opportunities; martial regime in Kurdish areas; and,
perhaps most viciously, "launching a vast anti-Kurdish campaign
amongst the Arabs," in accord with the official government program.
Syrian Kurdish political and religious leaders were arrested, deported,
or otherwise eliminated, and young Kurds were conscripted into the
Syrian armed forces with a special assignment to defend the Golan
Heights region on the frontier with Israel. The Syrian policy against
the Kurds is in keeping with the policies maintained by the Baath
against the Jews, and to a lesser extent, against the Syrian Druze.
As in the case in the other countries occupying Kurdistan, central
rule enforced through authoritarianism is the device utilized to project national unity and to preserve the revenues generated from the
oil and agricultural output of Syrian Kurdistan.

The situation confronting the Kurds over the past half century
exemplifies the manipulation of indigenous ethnonational, religious,
and linguistic groups in those Middle East states carved out of the
former Ottoman domain. The Kurds have been the most resilient of
the subnational groups fighting to preserve their collective unity and
national rights in the region. Their obfuscation by the governments
that rule them has been unsuccessful in extinguishing Kurdish national
sentiment. The policies of Iraq, Iran, Syria, and Turkey have, however, largely achieved their aims. These goals include presenting
their countries as consisting of united and homogeneous populaces
plagued only by Western imperialism and Zionism, which fosters such
"aberrations" as Kurdish national activity.

The Kurds, however, are not alone among the sad community
of submerged nationalities in the Middle East. The Armenians, Azer-

baijanis, Baluch, Druze, Turcomans, Maronites, Copts, Berbers, African Sudanese, and others confront a similar fate. The racialist system of government of the Middle East fosters the image that the region consists of a vast Arab core surrounded by the fraternal Islamic peoples of Turkey and Iran. This image, however, is tragically far from the truth.

6

BENEATH THE VEIL:
ARABIA-IN-AFRICA

Of the 150 million inhabitants of the states that comprise the
Arab League, two-thirds reside in northern Africa. The states in
which these 100 million "Arabs" reside include Algeria, Djibouti,
Egypt, Libya, Mauritania, Morocco, Somalia, and the Sudan. Additionally, there has been considerable international recognition of the
Saharan Arab Democratic Republic in the western Sahara. The pro-
ponents of this state are led by the Polisario, which has conducted a
guerrilla war supported by Libya and Algeria against Morocco for
control over the disputed territory.

The Arab states of northern Africa incorporate nearly 4 million
square miles, excluding lands unilaterally annexed from Chad by
Libya. This territory encompasses all of Africa north of, and including much of, the Saharan desert. It is a huge expanse of land dominat-
ing the gateway of Africa from the north and penetrating far into lands
inhabited throughout history by African blacks. In recent years, the
Arab countries in Africa have taken an increasingly activist role in
the Organization of African Unity and have been able to use that organization to promote distinctly Arab interests. This group of Arab
African states has been highly successful as a bloc in forcing a wedge
between Israel and black Africa, where a substantial amount of cooperation programs had previously existed.

It can be argued that some of the African Arab states are more
"Arab" than others. Egypt, for example, was the leading adversary
of Israel in the various wars waged by the Arabs against the Jewish
state, and Libya has, since the 1973 war, emerged as the single most
important bankroller of Arab terrorist groups. Additionally, Libya
and Algeria are at the forefront of the Arab Rejectionist and Steadfast
group of states, which a priori negates the possibility of coming to a

negotiated settlement with Israel. Libya has formed an Arab Liberation Army, the purpose of which has been the furtherance of Arab goals in Africa and in the Asian sector of the Middle East. From the standpoint of Arab political goals, the countries of northern Africa have been true champions of the Arab cause.

Ironically and significantly, many, perhaps most, of the inhabitants of the northern African countries that are identified as being "Arab" are not Arab in anything other than politics. African Arabdom is an idealized abstraction, which has a highly heterogeneous foundation of diverse racial, linguistic, religious, and ethnic groups. Egypt, perhaps the most "Arab" of the Arab states in Africa, has a numerically small, but indigenous Christian Coptic population which have, until the promulgation of President Anwar Sadat's relatively liberal policies, suffered considerable persecution and discrimination. In the post-Sadat era, Egyptian Copts fear a deterioration in their status.

In Somalia, a population consisting of the ethnically distinct and wretchedly poor Somali people live as part of the "Arab world." Somalia is a "frontline" Arab state, although the front that it defends is not the usual one, that with Israel, which is usually associated with the Arab world. Somalia is the frontal politico-military outpost of Arabdom against the "Abyssinians," that is, the black African Ethiopian state whose shore line on the Red Sea prevents total Arab control of that strategic waterway. Additionally, Somalia is an important springboard of activity pertaining to the struggle of Moslem secessionists attempting to wrest Eritrea from Ethiopia. Arab assistance of these insurgents potentiates the establishment of an additional state, an independent Eritrea, in the Arab orbit. Similarly, the former French territory of Afar and Issas, now known as Djibouti, has assumed an Arab identity despite the African ethnic and cultural heritage of that country's population.

Mauritania, literally "land of the Moors," is on the westernmost fringe of Arabia-in-Africa. The term "Moors" is an anthropological designation pertaining to populations of mixed Berber and Arab descent. Rounding northwestern Africa, on the coastlines, the cities of Casablanca, Rabat, Tangier, Tunis, Algiers, Tripoli, and Benghazi are eminently Arab centers. In the hinterlands of Morocco, Algeria, and Libya, however, the tribal, linguistic, and cultural ways of numerous Berber tribal federations and confederations are prevalent. There is no Arabdom in the Maghrebian interiors; Berber language, folkways, and social organization predominate in these areas. Aside from Egypt, only Tunisia has been able to fully Arabize its society, and the remnants of the indigenous Berber stock have been, in the main, totally obscured there.

The imposed Arabization that has taken place over much of northern Africa is not without its economic and other benefits to the

ruling elites of these countries. Many of these states have a history
of state formation similar to that of Arabia-in-Asia; that is, they were
composed to accord with the dictates of European imperial interests.
A country such as Libya previously consisted of three distinct units,
the Fezzan, Cyrenica, and Tripolitania, which were differentiated
from one another geographically, culturally, and administratively
throughout most of the pre- and post-Islamic periods. The same is
true of the other states in the Maghreb, but nowhere is this more
graphically the case as it is in the Sudan, where a state was forged
joining together dissimilar populations under a single national framework that has just barely survived.

SUDAN'S INTRINSIC SECTARIAN CLEAVAGES

In what has been referred to as "probably the most unreported
war in recent times," nearly 1.5 million Sudanese are reported to
have died as a direct or indirect result of the "Long War," which
nearly tore the country asunder during the period from 1955 to 1972.
The primarily pagan African population of the south was pitted against
the mainly Moslem and Arabic-speaking north in savage internecine
fighting, which had completely disrupted socioeconomic progress in
an already severely underdeveloped country. Sudan, with a total population of 17 million, 4.5 million of which is estimated to consist of
ethnic Africans (negroids), is the largest country on the continent,
being approximately the size of the United States east of the Missis-
sippi and larger than all of western Europe. It is a country of varied
terrains. Much of its territory is barren desert; however, some of the
richest soil in the world, perhaps the richest, is located there.
    The Sudan is presently a mosaic—formerly a cauldron—of vast
ethnic, linguistic, and religious variety. The northern six of Sudan's
nine provinces are Arabic speaking and Moslem, although there are
sharp tribal differences, as well as distinctions between sedentary and
nomadic groups. The southern region of the country has been self-
governing since the signing in March 1972 of the Addis Ababa Agreement, which ended the civil war between the Khartoum government and
the secessionists. The south is indigenously African, although its population derives from 572 tribes and subtribes. The majority of southern
Sudanese are pagans. A minority are Christians and, of these, most
are Roman Catholic. The religious organizational ties of these Christians with the West has been cited as a factor in the tensions and hostilities between the north and south. Such a simplistic analysis of the
situation does little, however, to clarify the myriad of problems that
has plagued the Sudan over the past century.
    As with most countries of the Arab world, the Sudan has no pre-

vious history of cohesive nationhood. The Sudan was a British dependency, the boundaries of which were drawn following a victory by the colonialists over native resistance to their rule. British colonialism was installed after the defeat of the Mahdist movement in 1898, which had been plaguing the British in their attempts to "pacify" Sudan. The idea of a mahdi, a deliverer/liberator of nearly messianic proportions in Islamic lore, has been prosecuted on a number of occasions in Africa and the Middle East by Moslems resisting foreign domination. The Mahdist movement of the 1880s, however, having set up a functioning state-like mahdiyya that warded off British advances for years, was no mere starry-eyed messianic movement. It was an effective utilization of religious fervor, anti-imperialist sentiment, and material resources that proved capable of staving off the forces of the strongest imperial power of the time. However, the mahdiyya was eventually defeated by British forces at the battles of Omduman and Khartoum under the leadership of Lord Kitchner.

The mahdiyya managed to unify much of northern Sudan against the British with an enduring passion for independence. This passion remains to this day in the form of the Ansar warrior movement of northern Sudan. Impeding the goals of the mahdiyya was another rival Moslem fundamentalist group: the Khatmiyya tribally based religio-political movement. Differences between the Ansaris and the Khatmiyya persist in the Sudan today.

The Mahdists were opposed to any foreign rule, including that of a Turco-Egyptian government, which was the first foreign domination that they rebelled against. British attempts at pacification were replaced in 1899 by the joint Anglo-Egyptian condominium, by which Egypt and Britain nominally controlled the Sudan jointly. The Mahdists were no less ill-disposed toward this form of administration than they were against outright British colonialism. Of course, since Britain ran Egypt as a virtual colony at the turn of the century, the Anglo-Egyptian condominium was little more than a thinly veiled form of colonial rule. The Khatmiyyas were not, however, as impassioned in their opposition to the Anglo-Egyptian condominium as were the Mahdists, and this, along with sectarian politics, eventually led to the divergent paths for the two major blocs of Arab Sudan.

As the Mahdist and Khatmiyya movements were developing in what is now northern Sudan, Christian missionaries were at work in the south. Many of the southern Sudanese tribes are ethnically related to populations in Uganda, Ethiopia, and Kenya, and it is in these tribal units that they trace their group identities. They reside on a fertile section of land, which is fed by the Nile waters. This fact of natural advantage eventually proved deleterious to the Sudanese Africans. The Nile was viewed by the British as the sole "highway" through the vast swampland known as the Sudd and the dense, unchartered brushland

of the country that led to central Africa. The Egyptian government
recognized that the control over the Nile waters would be critical to
its future agricultural development. Control over the Nile, therefore,
was an imperative for the British and the Egyptians. Accordingly,
access to the headwaters of the river was of the utmost necessity.
Control of the Nile headwaters demanded the territorial incorporation
of the previously distinct south Sudan. This was the economic underpinning for the otherwise incomprehensible grafting together of the
northern and southern Sudan into a gargantuan, unwieldy, and internally divided country.

The condominium continued over the Sudan into the early 1950s.
During the interim period, British and Egyptian technocrats, along
with a rising class of native, mostly Arab, Sudanese civil servants
governed the country. Two divergent development schemes were generated for this country: Arabic and Islam were encouraged in the north,
while the south was left to decay without benefiting from the infrastructure that was emerging in the north. This neglect of the south, and the
memory of the slave trade in which the Arabs had previously engaged,
along with the patronizing, discriminatory practices against them on
the part of the northerners, made the southern Sudanese skeptical concerning the creation of a new state in which they would be a minority
under a chauvinistically inclined Arab majority.

In the late 1940s, under the threat that they would have no say
whatsoever in the running of the nascent country, the southern Sudanese agreed to participate in a northern-dominated Legislative Assembly in preparation for imminent independence from the British. The
Legislative Assembly was dominated by the descendants of the Khatmiyya faction, which advocated, in the form of the National Union
Party, the union of the Sudan with Egypt in fulfillment of a vision of
the "Unity of the Nile Valley." The northerners predominated heavily
at the pre- and post-independence Legislative Assemblies, and the
National Union Party, in tacit cooperation with the militant Moslem
fundamentalist party (the Umma Party, led by the Ansaris), held a
virtual free reign over their country. As a result, Arabic culture,
language and officialdom was imposed on the south.

THE LIMITS OF ARABIZATION AND THE CIVIL WAR

By 1955, one year in advance of the date set for Sudan's inde-
pendence from Britain, a group of Southern military men mutinied.
This event is taken as the general departure point for the subsequent
Seventeen Year War between the north and south.

The southern viewpoint at its most conciliatory stance called
for the establishment of a federal form of government in the Sudan,

in which the various states would have considerable autonomy. Their parliamentary exercises toward this aim, which were doomed to failure owing to the domination by the northerners of the Legislative Assembly, were arrested entirely by the Arabist military coup in 1955, headed by General Ibrahim Abboud. The coup accelerated the development of militant activity in the south. With the dissolution of the Legislative Assembly and the proscription of political parties, the increasingly repressed southern leaders established various underground movements. These movements at first constituted a broad spectrum of organizations, owing to considerable personalist and tactical differences that arose among the leadership. In 1963 they shifted their strategy from a political to a military one, and the formation of the Anya-Nya guerrilla forces was achieved. During the subsequent nine years, the insurgents became a veritable army, under the command of General Joseph Lagu and other military and political leaders who banded together under one umbrella organization known as the Southern Sudan Liberation Movement.

The years of civil war wreaked havoc on the south. The region became a wasteland, strewn with the dead and dying, and the rudiments of an infrastructure that it did have smoldered under the crossfire between the southern and northern forces.

During the 1960s, there had been several changes in regime, alternating between civilian and military control. The present military government is led by General Gafar al-Nemiri, who came to power in 1969 as part of a leftist clique in opposition to the conservative policies of the Umma-led governments that preceded it.

A NEGOTIATED SETTLEMENT

Although juntas and the military are seldom known for their humanity and tolerance, the government of Gafar al-Nemiri has proved to be a godsend for the violence-wracked Sudan. Bringing a sensitivity to the southern problem unpossessed by any of his predecessors, Nemiri was able to conclude a negotiated settlement in 1972 with the Southern Sudan Liberation Movement, despite contrary pressures from the Arabist right. The basis of that settlement included regional autonomy for the southern provinces and amnesty for the freedom fighters of the Anya-Nya. The settlement paved the way for the national reconciliation that has characterized the Sudan since the war's conclusion.

From all indications, President Nemiri has been the only Arab leader to demonstrate any tolerance of the minority problem. This provides a double-edged sword, since many suspect that the tolerance and equality that Africans now receive in the Sudan will last only as long as Nemiri retains control over the country. There have been a number of coup attempts against Nemiri, and while his popularity has been strong, there is continuing dissidence against his government emanating from the right, in the form of the Ansars and the Moslem Brotherhood, as well as from the left, particularly from the Sudan Communist Party, which is among the strongest communist parties in Africa and the Middle East.

Much of what Nemiri has attempted to accomplish in national reconciliation has been subsidized by foreign aid. This aid, particularly that having to do with the development of an infrastructure, has been obtained from Western countries, notably the United States, Britain, and West Germany. The Arab countries have poured considerable sums of money into the country, but for the most part this has been devoted to the agricultural development of the Sudan. The motives behind the Arab's selective subsidization arises from Sudan's great potential as the "breadbasket" of the Arab world. Perhaps no other Arab country has the agricultural potential possessed by the Sudan. With the development of "Arab" agricultural resources, the Arab elites will be free from any threat of Western retaliation in response to future oil crises they may seek to create. The agricultural development of the Sudan is, therefore, an important enterprise as far as the Arab ruling elites are concerned. These elites have made their contributions to Sudan through the Kuwaiti Fund for Arab Economic Development and via similar channels.

Despite the positive basis for national reconciliation built by the Nemiri regime, north-south problems continue in the Sudan. Dedicated followers of the Anya-Nya movement remain, and in 1977 they announced the birth of a new "republic" in the Sudanese south. The "Genuine Movement for the National Independence of the Immantong Republic" had not, however, gained any discernable support from the southern Sudanese masses.

Further problems regarding national reconciliation have developed, both indigenous to the Sudan and emanating from foreign sources. There has been a price for Arab subsidization of Sudanese agriculture, forcing, for example, Nemeri to withdraw support for the Sadat peace initiative and otherwise loosening ties with Egypt, his erstwhile ally to the north. Additionally, there remains considerable Arabist, particularly Ansarist, sentiments in the north, and Nemiri's regime is perennially threatened by the now proscribed Communist Party.

It remains to be seen whether the marriage of the north and south of the Sudan can be sustained after the end of the Nemiri regime. As witnessed, however, by the "Long War," any attempt to impose Arabism or Islam on the citizens of the south will meet with entrenched resistance. The limits of Sudan's "Arabism" will be tested only at such time as the peaceful coexistence of the two communities will be threatened for the sake of wider Arab interests.

THE BERBERS ECLIPSED

The tragic bloodletting that characterized the Sudan prior to the advent to power of the Nemiri regime represents, along with the Armenian Massacre, the most extreme consequences of the Arabization of submerged groups in the Middle East. Less extreme, but nonetheless deleterious, is the cultural and linguistic obfuscation of other non-Arab groups residing in Arab states. The most concealed among such groups are the Berbers of Morocco, Algeria, and Libya. A search of even the best equipped libraries and research centers reveals the paucity of knowledge existing about this large ethnolinguistic group.

Owing to the struggle by the colonized peoples of northern Africa to overthrow the imperial yoke during the 1950s and 1960s, little attention has been paid to the internal differences within Maghrebian society by the outside world. The Arabization of the north African Berbers, however, is as symptomatic of the totalitarian uses to which pan-Arabism lends itself as any other manifestation of interethnic hostility in the Middle East. Though the consequences of Arabization in the Maghreb have been less severe in terms of loss of life and property than they have been in the Kurdish, Armenian, and African Sudanese cases, Arabization has been, nonetheless, resisted by the Berber populations of the area. Accordingly, the study of the attempts to obscure the existence of the Berbers is an important aspect of this study.

The term "Berber" refers to the linguistically and racially distinct peoples of the Maghreb. Their origins remain a mystery: their light skin and caucasoid features suggest that they are European in origin, as opposed to Semitic. Their language is a unique one of the Hamito-Semitic linguistic branch. Previously a pagan people, the Berbers adopted Islam at sword point in the seventh century as the tribes of Arabia swept out of the desert in order to spread their creed following the death of Mohammed. The Berbers of the Maghreb were both sedentary and nomadic, and until recently they were a dominantly tribal society. Consequently, entire tribes were converted to Islam in the early centuries of that religion's history.

BERBER RESISTANCE TO ARABIZATION

Despite their adoption of Islam, the Berbers vigorously resisted the Arabization of their society throughout the period following the Arab invasions. Nonetheless, the process of Arabization proceeded successfully in many parts of the Maghreb. In Tunisia, for example, there are no longer any exclusively Berber sections of the society. Nonetheless, Morocco and Algeria should, by demographic criteria, be designated "Berber" as opposed to "Arab" states.

The original adoption of the Islamic creed by the Berbers did not occur free of resistance. Although most Berbers today are Sunni Moslems, they had originally evolved a unique form of Islam. The Kharidjites (lit. "those who emerge from impropriety") came about in defiance of the Arab invasion of Tangiers in 739. The Kharidjite doctrine rebelled against the notion that the caliph had to be a descendant of Mohammed and thus be an Arab. There were other aspects of the sect's beliefs that challenged the paramountcy of the Arabs in their religious faith, and, in effect, expressed the importance of their identity as Berbers.

An infusion into the Maghreb of Arab tribes from Yemen during the twelfth to fourteenth centuries enhanced the influence of the Arabs throughout the area. These Arab tribes, though, were numerically in the minority of the societies that they dominated, and they were concentrated in the towns on the Mediterranean coastline. They intermarried with the Berbers of the coast and consequently a new derivation of the population, of mixed Arab-Berber blood, the Moors, came into existence. The Moors became the prevalent population of the coastline, but in the hinterland the Berbers remained, and do so today, the dominant social sector.

The role of the Berbers and the Moors in the spread of medieval Islamic culture was an important one. It was the Berber-led Almoravid and Almohad dynasties that imposed Islam on all of Morocco and reinforced it elsewhere in the Maghreb and Andalusia. There existed, however, a tension between traditional Berber folkways and the centralized authority that Islam began to impose on them through the caliphs. Some have described the Berbers as proto-anarchists in their political and social organization. They have traditionally regarded themselves as <u>imazighan</u> (free men), where authority and power was recognized on a highly decentralized basis.

A Berber's first loyalty is to the local canton, a collection of neighboring villages. Together cantons federate and form tribes, which in turn aggregate into tribal confederations. Each of these blocs have particularisms unique to their locale. Broadly speaking, one can distinguish groups of Berbers, linguistically and in terms of customs, as being of the Atlas, Rifian, Tuaregian, and other groups. As important as these differentiations are, however, those distinctions that divide the Berber town dweller from the mountain tribesman, and these from the desert nomad are equally significant.

While Berber identity is diffuse, the mobilization of large-scale Berber group alliances occurs in the face of an external, that is, non-Berber threat. These ad hoc alliances for the purpose of overcoming external threats are known as <u>leff</u> (pl. <u>elfuf</u>), and they are arrived at through the various stages of political practice and procedure that are unique to Berber society.

There is very little stratification in Berber society. Lands are cultivated collectively, and pasturage is viewed as belonging to the canton to which an individual Berber belongs. Each canton is ruled by a democratically elected assembly, the djemma, in which all male adults take part. The president of the djemma is the amin, who is generally viewed as the executor of the canton's collective will as expressed by the djemma. Additionally, under Ottoman administration, the Sublime Porte appointed an official, the gaid to oversee its interests within a group of tribes.

The djemma of one canton would agree to a leff with another canton in times of mutual duress, this being one of the ways in which a sense of Berber collectivity was maintained. Additionally, religious fraternities have been organized throughout the Maghreb in the form of lodges (zawia) that are founded in the locales of grave sites belonging to traditional Berber saints (marabouts).

The great premium placed by the Berbers on their independence and localism has given rise to the notion that there is no such thing as a unified Berber people. "Berber" is understood by many observers as simply being a linguistic designation, with little or no bearing on the polities under which various sectors of the Berbers reside. There is, accordingly, no basis for ethnic unity among Berbers in the opinion of some scholars. This is viewed as being particularly true in Algeria, where the battle lines drawn in that country's war of liberation divided Europeans from Moslems, rather than Berbers from Arabs. However, there have been examples in which uniquely Berber political interests were prosecuted. This can be observed both in Morocco and Algeria.

BERBER POLITICAL CULTURE

The first contemporary manifestation of Berber collectivity was the Rif Rebellion, led by the Berber leader Abdel Krim. Krim and his followers engaged nearly 70,000 Spanish troops during the 1920s in the Rif mountains of the Spanish zone of Morocco. In 1923 Krim had founded the Rif republic; he proclaimed its independence with himself as emir. The Rif republic, which lasted for over twelve months, resembled in a number of respects the Armenian republic of 1918-20. A number of government "ministries" were set up, and there were the rudiments of a diplomatic service and the beginnings of an infrastructure for a state apparatus. The demise of the Rif republic, however, was found in the political division of the Berber population between the French and Spanish zones. While Krim maintained the support of Berbers in the Spanish zone, the French had been able to secure the allegiance of Berbers living in their sphere of control. Consequently, when the Rifians were drawn into battle with the French and were in need of support from the Berbers of their zone, they were undone and the republic collapsed. However, the Rif republic did demonstrate the strength, as well as the ultimate weakness, of Berber cohesiveness.

Other expressions of Berber solidarity, or at least consciousness, existed in the "Berber crisis" of 1949, when a split developed in the Mouvement pour le Triomphe des Libertes Democratiques (MTLD) over the issue of Algeria's Arabism. An important, albeit small section of the party objected to the Arabization of the movement and adamantly called for the ethnic unity of all Algerian Muslims—Arabs, Berbers, and Turks—in the fight against the French. While the crisis was resolved with a minimum of enmity, it set the path for subsequent efforts by the liberation movement and the government to increase the use of Arabic language in Algerian society. Algerian Berbers were, and remain, not interested in viewing their country as an Arab state, preferring instead to view themselves as Algerians, or if part of any extraterritorial community, as Moslems.

Despite their avowed attempts to make Algeria a nonsectarian state, the Algerian government was forced to put down insurrections shortly after independence in the Kabyle mountains, where the country's 3 million Berbers are to be found. The denial of official status to Berber language was the primary source of discontent among the Kabyle at that time.

Similarly, riots in the Kabyle region as well as in Algiers came about in April 1980 after the Algerian government refused to lift the restrictions on the use of Berber language and culture. There appears to be a growing concern among Berbers that their country is presently more a vehicle for pan-Arabism than an instrument of its indigenous population. The Berber outburst occurred immediately after protests by pan-Arabist-oriented students and Islamic fundamentalists in eastern Algeria during January 1980, as well as in reaction to comments by Algerian President Chadli Benjedid affirming his government's "faith in our Arabness." This was followed in the summer of 1980 by statements made by Colonel Muammar Qadaffi of Libya that Berbers were really Arabs and that to maintain differently was to engage in "colonialist culture." Qadaffi apparently made these statements after having pronounced the Berbers in his country, the Tuaregs, to be "Arabs."

More subtle, but nonetheless potentially potent, evidence of a latent Berber discontent with the Arab governments under which they reside are to be found in Morocco, particularly in the coup attempt of July 1971. The activities of the Berbers on behalf of Moroccan independence were considerable. However, the call by the Moroccan nationalists that all ethnic and linguistic distinctions be submerged under an Arab identity aroused a number of Berber intellectuals to anxiety and irredentism. The discontent was quieted, however, by the cooptation of the Berbers by King Hassan II, who structured his military in such a way that various arms of the army became solely Berber. In later years, the "Berberist" Mouvement Populaire (MP) became the repository of the Berber constituency, lobbying against the Arabist orientation of the dominant Istaqlal (Independence) party and in favor of the use of Berber in schools located in Berber areas. The successes of the MP, which has been identified as a rightist party, have been minimal. The Berber overrepresentation in the military had succeeded in placating Berber traditionalists for a time.

However, dissatisfaction with the inherent limits to Berber involvement in the Moroccan power structures was a contributing factor in the attempted palace coup in July 1971. The attempted coup was not exclusively a Berber affair. However, since the coup against the throne of King Hassan II, a sherrifian Arab, was executed by senior officers, the overwhelming majority of whom were Berbers, there is some coincidence of ethnic dissidence and frustration on the part of the military. As a result of the coup attempt, Hassan has had to reorder his court and reallocate power. He has steered toward a more Arabist course, utilizing, for example, more Arabic in his public speech, rather than the more commonly used idiom of French. Politically, he has identified his country more closely with the Arab camp in an effort to stave off the leftist opposition that continues to grow against him. In a further effort to prolong what many consider to be his numbered days, King Hassan has preoccupied his country, including the Berber elite, with the "national duty" of seizing the western Saharan.

The memory of the infamous dahir Berbere, promulgated by the French in 1930 in an attempt to coopt the Berbers and divide them from Arab Moroccans, lingers preeminently in the minds of Maghrebian intellectuals. Throughout the past century, the "enemy" has been the Europeans, not other north African minorities. Both Berber and Arab intellectuals agree on this.

The toll of European imperialism on the minds, bodies, and souls of the north Africans was immense in scope, and it is from this imperialism that north Africa still reels. It is an imperative of the new Algeria and Morocco that state legitimacy be established, and any unnecessary cleavages must therefore be overlooked. The Berbers, to a great extent, are apparently willing to abide by such attempts at national unity. The emergence, however, of an order that places one ethnolinguistic group above another bears the very seeds of nationalist self-destructions that the Maghrebian nationalists fear. Until now, such hegemonism has not occurred. However, the veering toward Arabism at the expense of cultural parity between the Berber and Arab sectors will promote increased dissidence and erode the foundations of future Maghrebian regimes. This is attested by the recent riots in Algiers and rumblings elsewhere in the Maghreb.

7

ARMENIA:
ELUDING NATIONAL EXTINGUISHMENT

In the period since the Enlightenment, few acts of human design have proved as calamitous and tragic as the massacre of 1.5 million Armenians during World War I. The decimation of this ancient people nearly resulted in their elimination from the family of nations. Further, as the victims of one of the two or three attempted genocides of this century, the Armenians have not been the beneficiaries of any reparations or recompensation.

While the existence of a Soviet Armenian Republic has provided some possibility for national reconstruction, bitterness and frustration continue to plague the Armenian diaspora. Consequently, the recent attacks launched by the Armenian Liberation Army and other clandestine forces operating in the name of the Armenians express opposition to the status quo that has been foisted upon the Armenian community. The massacre and other acts of persecution against the Armenians were implemented by the Ottomans. Therefore, representatives of the contemporary Turkish republic are the primary targets of Armenian revenge. In order to comprehend the deep-seated enmity felt by the Armenians toward the Turks, it is important to appreciate the status of the Armenians under the Ottomans.

The Christians posed a serious problem to the Ottomans, since Islam was the legitimizing formula that permitted the caliph to preside over his empire as he wished. The most problematic of these Christians were the Armenians, a people whose national existence preceded the birth of Islam by thousands of years. Additionally, the Armenians had resided in Asia Minor, the seat of the Ottoman sultanate, since their formation as a cogent national group. The tenacity with which they retained their unique national identity and the memory of the national freedom they had enjoyed under sovereign Armenian rulers further threatened the sultanate.

Ethnically, the Armenians are the result of the intermingling of indigenous Hurrian tribes with an Indo-European group that migrated into Asia Minor 3,000 to 3,500 years ago.

The Armenian language, like Persian, is a branch of the Indo-European linguistic group. Its usage is restricted solely to the Armenian nation, since further propagation was prevented by the geographic, cultural, and later religious isolation of the Armenian nation from the surrounding peoples. Like Arabic, there are regional dialects in spoken Armenian, and literary Armenian differs from the vernacular. An alphabet, unique to the Armenian language, was devised by Saint Merop Mashtotz in the fifth century. A considerable body of literary material in the Armenian tongue has developed throughout the centuries.

In religion, the Armenians have demonstrated a singularity of view and practice. Previously pagan and Zoroastrian, the Armenians became the first nation to embrace Christianity en bloc in the fourth century. Their sect of Christianity was rendered even more uncommon after the split that followed the Council of Chaledon in 451 A.D. While 90 percent of the Armenians subscribe to the Orthodox Armenian Church, there are other Armenian Christian denominations, including an Armenian Catholic Church, and the Armenian Evangelical Church. Additionally, within the Orthodox Church a schism took place in 1932 over a political incident dividing different political parties within the Armenian community.

The role of religion in Armenian national life is an important one. As for the Jews, religion represents the repository of the national will in the diaspora and the chief form of national expression. In the diaspora, the church acts as the center of the Armenian community's activities. As the community's focus, the Armenian Church has an ethnocultural function that differentiates it from the Christian denominations of the West. The churches of the Middle East—the Maronite, the Coptic, the Armenian, and the Assyrian—all share a similar ethnonational function.

The unique national identity of the Armenians has continued throughout their turbulent political history. Since the rise of Islam and especially during the Ottoman reign, the Armenians had been subjected to various forms of harassment and persecution. It is only with the development of a reconstituted homeland in the Soviet Union that the Armenians have been able to recapture some measure of autonomy and free national expression. The historical process leading to the establishment of the Soviet Armenian Republic fluctuated between the darkest hours of pogrom and genocide to the glory of resistance and national rebirth. The genocide was a result of the convulsions endured by the dying Ottoman Empire. In effect, the persecution and ultimate massacre of the Armenian community represented the extent of decay to which the Ottoman Empire finally succumbed during World War I.

THE ARMENIANS UNDER ISLAM

The political conditions that gave rise to the use of the Armenians as a scapegoat for Ottoman tyranny assumed religious colors during the early periods of Ottoman control. A primary problem afflicting non-Moslems of the empire was the status of the dhimmis, a discriminatory status to which the Christians and Jews are subjected under Koranic law. A factor in the persecution of the Armenians that was of equal if not greater importance than their status as dhimmis was the organizational ties between the Armenians and the Christian powers of Europe. The European powers maintained imperial designs on the Christian parts of the Ottoman Empire, including the Balkans, the Bosphoros, and Thrace.The Armenians and other Christians of the empire were, therefore, always regarded as a potential "fifth column" that might betray the Ottomans in the interests of the European powers.

Additionally, from a geostrategic point of view, Armenia stands as a kind of natural fortress between Europe and Asia. Ottoman control of Armenia was necessary to ward off any potential European invasion from the west or Romanov invasion from the north. Therefore, the retention of Armenia as part of the Ottoman inheritance was considered imperative. Strict control over the population of the territory was, accordingly, mandatory. The subjugation of the Armenian people was elevated to a requirement of state if the empire were to remain intact.

The introduction by the sultanate of the millet system in the fourteenth century, whereby the internal affairs of minority communal life were self-governed with minimal intervention from the Ottoman authorities, permitted the Armenians some measure of autonomy. They continued the use of their language and traditional lifestyle. Compared to the other non-Moslem minority communities, the status of the Armenians was, for much of the time, no worse than it was for the other minorities.

The nineteenth century, however, brought about a rapid deterioration in the status of the Armenian community. While the millet system provided for the survival of Armenian heritage, the Armenian community was resourceless with respect to facilities necessary to protect itself. Beginning with the Russian-Persian War of 1828, which resulted in a considerable amount of eastern Armenia being usurped and placed under Romanov control the decimation of Armenia and the persecution of the Armenian people commenced.

The harassment of Christians and the interethnic tensions that began in the 1830s prompted the protest of the European powers, who were looking for any pretext to exercise influence over the Ottomans in view of the geostrategic importance of the lands under the sultan's reign. When Turkey signed the Treaty of Adrianople in 1829, it vowed to protect Christian minorities. When such protection failed to materialize, the Europeans demanded greater Ottoman reform, which was agreed to in the sultan's decree (the Hatti Sherrif) of 1839. The decree officially expunged all institutionalized forms of discrimination against the Christian minorities. The decree, however, had little material affect if any, and another declaration affirming the equality of all Ottoman subjects was issued in 1856, again at the insistence of the European powers. The Europeans accepted the declaration at face value; however, they had other interests motivating them to seek cooperation with the Ottomans, and they did not make such cooperation contingent on the actual implementation of the sultan's decree. In 1856 the Treaty of Paris was signed by the Ottomans and the European governments in which the latter agreed "not to interfere, whether collectively or separately, in the relations of His Majesty the Sultan with his subjects or in the internal administration of his Empire." In the succeeding years, Moslem and Durze persecution of Lebanese Christians forced the latter's flight to the cities. In 1860, 11,000 Christians were massacred in their ghetto in Damascus. Obviously, the fact that the European powers had relinquished their influence over the sultan on the matter of his Christian subjects contributed to this atrocity.

ARMENIA AND THE SUPERPOWERS

The dismemberment of the Ottoman Empire proceeded at a fast pace. The Balkan states had been surrendered, and with the surrender of Ottoman control over Bulgaria and Macedonia, the European holdings of the Ottoman state were terminated. The Russians went to war against the Ottomans in 1878 as a result of its territorial designs on the empire as well as in the defense of Christians living under the Turks. Two treaties terminated the hostilities between the countries. The Treaty of San Stefano (March 1878) made particular mention of the Armenians, stating that the Ottoman regime would insure the well-being of the Armenian community against the attacks of the Moslems. However, the Treaty of Berlin (June 1878), in which the Russians dictated the terms for the termination of the Russo-Turkish War, superseded the San Stefano accord and made the protection of Armenian rights dependent on the withdrawal of Russian troops from the areas of Turkish Armenia they occupied. The British acquiesced to this abandonment of the Armenians in an attempt to curry favor with the Ottomans, whose cooperation was then being sought by the British in their campaign to achieve hegemony in the Middle East over French and Russian competition. Turkey returned Britain's flirtations, and Britain received Cyprus as a reward for its protection of Turkish interests during the challenge posed to them by the Russians. Armenian rights were, therefore, sacrificed by the Russian withdrawal from Armenia and by the British–Ottoman quid pro quo. The acquisition of the new British Crown Colony of Cyprus was exchanged for British cooperation in effecting the withdrawal of Russian troops from Ottoman lands. The British rapprochement with the Turks and other superpower machinations were carried out at the neglect of Armenian security. This set the stage for the first genocidal campaign exercised by the Ottomans against the Armenians, which took place in the last quarter of the nineteenth century. This genocide was implemented under the sultanate of Abdul-Hamid II and his successors, the Young Turks, as a means by which popular discontent over government policies could be diverted.

Throughout the late nineteenth century, the Ottoman Empire played an increasingly important role in the imperial enterprise of the European powers. The geostrategic importance of the lands over which the sultan ruled was of great significance to the British and French and later to the Germans and Italians as well. Imperial interests overtook moral issues as well as Christian solidarity and international agreements. The Ottomans were free to use the Armenians as a scapegoat, and regular pogroms against them were carried out by nonofficial paramilitary units who operated with the tacit encouragement of the sultan. The drumbeat of genocide would increase with German involvement in Ottoman affairs.

Rapidly industrializing Germany, as well as France and Britain, were in search of new territorial spheres of influence in order to obtain natural resources and strategic markets needed to bolster their economies. The Russians and the Italians, not to be outdone by their rival colonial powers, were also seeking new domains in order to support their tottering regimes. There was a grand race being conducted by the European colonial powers, and the quest for colonial possessions and dependencies assumed the imperative of state survival. Further, battle lines were being drawn in this race for colonies, and new alliances created strange bedfellows among the imperial powers.

The British had been making steady inroads in the Islamic east, both as a tactical necessity for the maintenance of firm control over India, as well as for purposes of gaining ascendancy in the hitherto unexploited Middle East. The French had also done moderately well in their attempt to gain advantage in the Moslem lands of northern Africa and in Syria and Lebanon. The traditional rivalries of the two main metropolitan powers of France and England were submerged during this period in light of the renewed vigor with which the Russians and Germans raced for colonies. The speed with which the new upstart, Germany, began to assert itself in acquiring holdings, in shoring its military and naval capacities, and in successfully influencing the non-industrialized countries startled the French, British, and Russians, since Germany had not previously been regarded as a serious rival. The French, British, and Russians eventually formed the Triple Entente, in which it was understood that the colonial designs of the individual countries could only be accomplished through concerted efforts to defeat the rival imperial constellation, the emerging Triple Alliance (Germany, Italy, and Austro-Hungary). The struggle for hegemony between the French and British was not forgotten; it was merely subordinated to the greater tactical concerns of the hour.

It had become increasingly obvious to Kaiser Wilhelm II that his success in rising to the top of the colonial ladder was contingent on the achievement of a solid footing in the Near East, the gateway to the Orient. At the time, the Ottoman Empire was exercising nominal control over the Arabs, Kurds, Berbers, and other Moslem peoples of the Middle East. An administrative framework for the rule of these peoples was already existent, one which the kaiser could coopt and utilize in his efforts to outmaneuver the British, French, and Russians. The Ottoman Empire was coextensive with much of the Moslem world, and therefore the forging of ties with Sultan Abdul-Hamid and the consolidation of his control over the empire were considered central to the strategic interests of the German Empire.

Germany emerged as Turkey's "friend and protector" or, perhaps, its master. Considerable monies were spent by the Germans in the rehabilitation of the Turkish army and in the construction of a railroad that would unite the German and Ottoman empires. The Turks realized that a strong relationship with the Germans was necessary on two counts: (1) both the Germans and the Turks had a common interest in seeing the British and French lose influence in the Middle East, since the former's presence there greatly weakened the Ottoman Empire and prevented the Germans from extending their empire into the region; and (2) any weakening of the Ottoman state would strengthen the Russian Empire and afford it the possibility of annexing the Bosphoros and other sections of the Ottoman Empire bordering the Black Sea. By the time that the Committee of Union and Progress had gained control of the empire, the Ottomans had inherited an inescapable dependence on the Germans from Sultan Abdul-Hamid.

Underdevelopment, the same process that brought the Ottoman Empire into the German imperial fold, was also responsible for the rapidly falling fortunes of the Turkish state. The infusion of German capital and expertise did not alleviate the difficulties faced by Ottoman subjects. The sultan's popularity was quickly waning, and the disaffection of the Ottoman masses was, with Abdul-Hamid's tacit approval, blamed on the Armenians. Eventually the plight of the Armenians would grow so desperate that a phase of armed resistance was entered into

by Armenian nationalists. This resistance began concurrently with
the start of the Armenian genocide.

THE ARMENIAN RESISTANCE

In August 1896, a group of nationalists of the Dashnaktsoutune
(the Dashnak, the Armenian Revolutionary Federation) launched a bold
attack on the Ottoman Bank in Constantinople. The aim of the lightning
attack was the securing of assurances from the Western powers that
they would hold the Ottomans to their vows concerning the upholding
of Armenian rights. The Dashnaks secured guarantees from the European ambassadors, who also provided the Armenian nationalists with
safe conduct out of Turkey. Subsequently, however, the Western powers had either committed an act of the most vile perfidy or were truly
unable to control the Ottomans: in the days following the attack on the
Ottoman Bank, 300,000 Armenians were slaughtered in the Turkish
capital beneath the gaze of European diplomats stationed there.

The Armenian resistance had been organized into a cogent movement in 1890, when several different groups of Armenian nationalists
had come together to form the Dashnaktsoutune, an organization that,
despite a considerable change in program, still exists. The organization would eventually play a critical leadership role in the numerous
acts of resistance preceding and during the 1915 Armenian Massacre.

In the summer of 1908, under the banner of "equality, justice
and fraternity," the Young Turks of the Committee for Union and Progress (Ittahad Ve Terraki) dethroned Sultan Abdul-Hamid and introduced a constitution. The event aroused great optimism among Armenians, who believed that the long awaited reforms would finally be implemented under the new regime. The sultanate of Abdul-Hamid had
been among the bloodiest ever experienced in the history of the Armenians, and so the Young Turks and their projected constitution were
welcomed by the Armenians, especially since the reforms that were
to be implemented were a development indigenous to the Ottoman Empire, one that did not require the benevolence and actions of external
powers. Despite the promise that the Young Turks' ascendancy held
for the Armenians, 30,000 of them were put to death in the city of
Adana within one year of the Committee of Union and Progress's rise
to power.

By April 1909, Abdul-Hamid was finally deposed, exiled, and
replaced by his younger brother, Sultan Mohammed V. The empire,
however, continued its decay. Chief among its losses was the independence of Bulgaria and Montenegro and the union of Crete with
Greece. Additionally, Italy usurped Tripolitania and other territorial
holdings of the sultanate in north Africa. The annexation resulted from

an understanding reached between France, Great Britain, and Italy, which apportioned various parts of the Ottoman domain to each other as the empire disintegrated. Italy eventually achieved its territorial ambitions through force, having defeated the Turkish army during the Italian-Turkish War in 1911.

The taxing of the Ottoman resources engendered by the Italian-Turkish and the Balkan Wars of 1912 placed the Committee of Progress and Unity and their subjects in a state of angry agitation. The Armenians again assumed the role of a defenseless scapegoat, betrayed by the European powers, which remained absorbed in their strategic schemes. After appealing to the powers once more, during the conference leading to the Treaty of London (which officially concluded the Balkan Wars), and having been treated there to a deafening silence, the Armenians turned to their northern neighbor, the Russians, for assistance. The Russians obliged and, on June 8, 1913, submitted a memorandum to the European powers demanding that they insure Ottoman compliance with a number of reforms agreed to but not yet implemented by the Ottomans.

After a prolonged and arduous series of negotiations, an agreement was reached between the Russian ambassador (de facto representing the European powers) and the grand vizier (prime minister) of Turkey on February 8, 1914. The agreement stipulated that the Armenian provinces were to be divided into two parts, each of which was to be placed under the supervision of two European inspector generals, a Dutch and Norwegian. They were to administer the provinces and insure adherence to the related terms of the agreement, which guaranteed the full equality of Armenians and Turks under the law, the unfettered use of the Armenian language and its admissibility as an official public language, the representation of the Armenians in the General Councils governing the country, and the taking of an annual census so that the growth of the Armenian population could be monitored and their needs catered to.

The inspector generals had not yet arrived in Armenia when World War I broke out. At that time, the Young Turks promptly renounced the agreement with the Russians and arrogantly resumed their policy of repression against the Armenians.

The Young Turks were committed to a policy of pan-Turanianism, whereby all the Turkish-speaking peoples of the empire and Transcausasia would be united under one regime. This policy portended trouble for the Christians, non-Turkish Armenians.

GENOCIDE OF THE ARMENIANS

As Russian involvement in the war seemed increasingly likely, and in an effort to consolidate their internal forces, the Young Turks

made direct overtures to the Dashnak, offering autonomy under a
Turkish protectorate if the Armenians would assist in resisting any
attack on Turkey by Russia. The Dashnak rejected the Turkish request and advised its people to steer neutral of any involvement in
World War I. Further, it adopted a resolution urging the Turkish
government not to enter the war. Sectors of the Armenian nations
were to be found on both sides of the Turkish/Russian border, and
thus it was argued that taking sides would inevitably jeopardize one
of the sectors of Armenia. While this was sound reasoning, the
Armenian nation was subsequently victimized beyond belief by its refusal to fight with the Turks against the Russians. The Armenian
strategy of neutrality was converted by the Ottoman propaganda machine as being indicative of Armenian support for the Russians. This,
coupled with the participation of thousands of Russian Armenians in
the Russian armies provided the necessary pretext for the all-out
genocide against the Armenians carried out by the Turks in the second
year of World War I.

Rumors, which were said to originate with Enver Pasha, the
Turkish minister of war, alleged that the Turkish Armenians had
aligned themselves with, and were fighting alongside, the Russians
against the Turks. It was for this reason, the rationale went, that the
Turkish forces were then losing the war on the Caucasus front. The
liquidation of the Armenian population on the pretense that they were
traitors was put forth. This gave the Turks a scapegoat that could
turn attention away from its own inadequacies and provided an excuse
by which the annoying Armenian question could be ended once and for
all.

The debauchery that followed resulted in the outright murder of
1 million of the 2.5 million Armenians living under the Turks and
death due to starvation, disease, or exposure of another 500,000 Armenians. In June 1915, in accordance with plans that may have been
formulated as early as 1913, Armenian soldiers serving in the Turkish military were ordered to hand over their weapons. Within a month,
the conscription age for Armenian men was extended to include all
Armenians between the ages of 15 and 60. The next stage of the nascent genocide involved the arrest in April of 1,000 prominent Armenian leaders in Constantinople. Taken to the interior of the country,
the Armenian leaders were murdered. This was the beginning of the
1915 Armenian Massacres.

The Armenian soldiers in the Turkish army were constituted
into "Armenian Labor Battalions," which were the vehicles by which
these men literally paved the way to their own death. Systematically,
males of a given Armenian village were ordered to appear in the central square at an appointed time. When they presented themselves, the
men would be formed into long columns, tied one to another, and told

that they were being marched to Baghdad, Mosul, or some other point south and east of Armenia. Similarly, women, children, and the infirm would be gathered and told that they were being resettled, evacuated out of Armenia where their lives, they were informed, were jeopardized. Few of those "evacuated" ever made it to the desert areas to which they were being led, and those who did arrive soon died, owing to the lack of water, food, and shelter. In essence, these were death marches; the men would be actively massacred, while the women were left to the ravages of starvation, thirst, and fatigue.

The atrocities suffered by the Armenian people in the annus terribilis of 1915 is unrivaled in modern history except for the Nazi's war against the Jews. Obviously, the German mentors of the Ottoman High Command were able to gain considerable experience in the creation of concentration camps, slave labor, and genocide from their field experiences in the campaign against the Armenians. The Armenian genocide was witnessed and documented by numerous observers: the account of the massacre as described by the U.S. ambassador to Constaninople has been made into a book entitled Ambassador Morgenthau's Story. Arnold Toynbee has also provided documentation in his work, The Treatment of Armenians in the Ottoman Empire.

THE UNFOLDING OF ARMENIAN NATIONALISM

When at the end of the war, the smoke cleared and the death tally taken, the carnage suffered by the Armenian people became horribly clear. Russian Armenians were permitted to provide shelter and assistance to the survivors of the Turkish Armenian genocide, and a considerable number of refugees were absorbed. While Russian troops remained in Caucasia, they arrested the attempts by the Turks to continue the slaughter of Armenian survivors. After the Russian Revolution, however, the reorganization of the Russian army left the Armenians—those who had been Russian subjects and those who were refugees—exposed to the seasoned Turkish troops. Under the leadership of the Dashnaks, the Armenians rapidly formed fighting units that, though without benefit of military training and adequate matériel, kept the Turks at bay for five months. Despite this bold resistance, whenever an advance was made by the Turks, the civilians and the fighting units of the Armenian community, the fedayee, in the Russian zone, would pay dearly.

At the conclusion of the war, though subjected to superpower perfidy, Armenian independence was recognized on a sliver of historic Armenia. The Armenian republic of 1918–20 and later the establishment of Soviet Armenia became the vehicles for the preservation and rehabilitation of Armenian national existence.

The short-lived Armenian republic came about on a fragment of Armenia that had been temporarily neglected by the Russians and Turks. The withdrawal of Russian troops from Armenia in mid-1916 was, ironically, a result of Russian confidence concerning the imminent defeat of the Turks. Russian incorporation of Turkish Armenia had apparently been decided upon in a quid pro quo that had been pre-arranged by the Triple Entente. France was to receive Cilica and the westernmost part of the Armenian plateau, the British were to glean most of Mesopotamia and inland Syria, and the Russians were to get the hinterland of Armenia. Since this was already decided, Russian appeasement of Armenian grievances was no longer necessary, nor was the protection of the Armenians incumbent upon the tsar. Armenia was to be incorporated into the Romanov Empire, and the tsar would do with it as he wished, including, perhaps, repopulating it with Cossacks and Georgians. With international recognition of his sovereignty over Armenia, and the concomitant free hand that the powers had granted to one another as part of their carving up Asia Minor and Transcaucasia, the tsar feared nothing concerning the Armenians. He was now free to remove the military support that had buffered the Armenians from the Turks.

It was therefore not surprising that the Armenians, like the Transcaucasian mountaineers and the Georgians, welcomed the downfall of the Romanov Empire. The tsar's nationalities policy was treacherous to say the least, and the belief that Sovietization would be translated into liberalization and decentralization fired the spirits of the Transcaucasian peoples. These peoples formed an administrative unit, the Ozakom, for the purposes of developing the denuded region. The Ozakom never accomplished its aims due to the paucity of resources available to it, and consequently the Armenians again started looking toward a suitable form of government of their own. An Armenian National Congress was convened, and an Armenian National Council was formed as the executive arm of nascent Armenian administration in Transcaucasia. The Transcaucasian peoples presented a united delegation to the Petrograd All-Russian Constituent Assembly. As events unfolded, the assembly was dispersed per order of the Bolshevik leadership in January 1918, which had declared the establishment of the Soviet Union only a few months earlier.

The pretext used by the Soviets in withdrawing their troops from Armenia was that their presence prevented Armenian self-determination. Additionally, in order to placate the anxious Moslems under its rule, the Bolsheviks were interested in demonstrating that they entertained no territorial claims to Moslem Asian lands that was not already under their control.

Caught between the belief that they would one day be part of a federative democratic republic founded on the lands of the Russian

Empire and refusing to recognize the Bolshevik seizure of power, the Transcaucasian peoples, including the Armenians, found themselves in the unenviable position of governing themselves despite the profound lack of available resources. They recognized that Transcaucasia had to make peace with the Ottomans, if the latter were to be prevented from subjugating the entire region. The cost of a permanent peace was made clear to the Transcaucasians by the Young Turks: Turkish Armenia would have to be ceded to Turkey. The cooperative Transcaucasian administrative unit was extremely weak, and acquiescence to the Turkish demands was inevitable. Despairingly, but realistically, the Armenians resigned themselves to the fact that there would not be a united Turkish-Russian Armenia.

The Ottomans' position on Armenia had been confirmed by negotiations with the Bolsheviks and the still independent Ukrainians. These negotiations, which eventually led to the Treaty of Brest-Litovsk, ceded large tracts of Armenia to the Turks, much more than had been previously agreed. The Transcaucasians had refused to recognize the Bolshevik administration, but the Bolsheviks had been willing to surrender the Armenian Transcaucasian districts of Kars, Batum, and Ardahan to Turkey. Therefore, the Turks went for the hardest bargain possible and, in their negotiations with the Transcaucasians, demanded that the Treaty of Brest-Litovsk be the basis of the peace. Further eroding the unity of the Transcaucasian peoples was the willingness of the Azerbaijanis and other Islamic peoples of the region to capitulate to the Turkish demands in the name of Moslem solidarity and pan-Turkish vision. Christian/Moslem fighting broke out in Transcaucasia and further exacerbated the difficulties.

The Christian Transcaucasians, which included the Georgians and the Armenians, recognized that a peace made on Ottoman terms was completely contrary to their desire for self-determination, and, therefore, they declared war against the Ottoman state. In the spring of 1918, the Ottomans had quickly overtaken Turkish Armenia and encroached on Russian Armenia and Georgia. The Georgians and Transcaucasian mountaineers called for the submergence of the various national groups into a single Transcaucasus Federative Republic in order to repulse the Turks and retain some fraction of self-determination. On the one hand, a response to this call for a multinational republic would not provide for Armenian independence. Additionally, the fortress province of Kars was firmly in the hands of Armenian fighting forces, and indications were that the Armenians could hold the area against the Turkish onslaught and achieve independence if the other Transcaucasian peoples would assist them. The Georgians, however, particularly needed the Federative Republic if they were to enjoy any measure of freedom, and certainly they would not cooperate with an independently administered Armenia at the cost of the Federative Republic. Therefore, lacking any other option, the Armenians were forced to compromise and join in the formation of the Transcaucasus Federative Republic, which declared its independence in April 1918.

The government of the Transcaucasus Federative Republic prepared to accept peace with the Turks on the basis of the Treaty of Brest-Litovsk in return for recognition and peace. Much to the disbelief of the Transcaucasians, however, the Ottomans again amended their demands, stating that further territorial concessions were required before there could be peace between neighbors.

At this point, a divergence of German and Turkish interests emerged. The Germans had concluded a peace agreement with the Soviets calling for German abandonment of territorial designs on Transcaucasia in return for a steady supply of raw materials from the area. The Turks, on the other hand, sought to expand their governance over Transcaucasian land, thus potentiating a strain in the fragile German-Soviet relationship. The Germans were unable to exercise any influence over the intractable Turks. Their strategy turned, therefore, to the conclusion of an accord with the Georgians and the achievement of an understanding with the Azerbaijanis that called for the creation of Georgian and Azerbaijani republics. These republics would be protected by the Germans. This would, of course, require the dissolution of the Transcaucasian republic. Within weeks of its independence, the Transcaucasian republic was dissolved. Faced with Turkish encroachment, deprived of Soviet cooperation, and confronted with the loss of the Transcaucasian framework, the Armenian National Council was forced to declare the independence of the Armenian republic, totally unexpectedly, on May 28, 1918. The requisite first order of business was the attainment of a modus vivendi with the despised Turks.

THE REPUBLIC OF ARMENIA

With independence foisted upon them, the Armenians had at once to assume the responsibility of state, while at the same time conducting a defensive war against the Turks and, all the while, seeking peace with them. Spontaneous battles arose, and it began to appear that the Armenians had not only repulsed the Turkish attacks, but they would have forced the Turks out of all of Russian Armenia had it not been for the achievement of a peace accord with Constantinople. On June 4, 1918, the Treaty of Peace and Friendship was signed by the representatives of the Turkish government and the republic of Armenia. The treaty involved the establishment of the Armenian republic on a mere 4,400 square miles of land. Additionally, it called for the immediate reduction of the Armenian armed forces. The terms of the treaty included demands for the expulsion of all nationals whose governments were hostile to the Central Powers, called for constitutional guarantees of Muslim civil liberties, and demanded the provision of a strategic carte blanche to the Ottomans, permitting them to march troops and supplies across the republic as they wished. These were the conditions for "peace" between the Armenian republic and the Turks.

The republic had been proclaimed out of necessity. It lacked, however, the basic elements of government. Without a civil infrastructure, the Armenian republic was immediately beset with the burden of a great mass of Armenian refugees who were in immediate need of rehabilitation.

Compounding the difficulties and disorganization that plague most new countries, Armenia had to contend with the continuation of Turkish-German designs concerning the Baku oil field on the Caspian shore. Throughout the summer of 1918, the Germans and the Turks strove to capture this strategically important city. In September 1918, Armenian resistance finally broke down in Baku, resulting in the takeover of the city by the Turks. As a result, 30,000 Armenian lives were lost, having been massacred by the victorious Turks.

The Armenian republic was led throughout its two-year existence by the Armenian Revolutionary Federation, the Dashnak, which had remained the preeminent Armenian party. Lesser parties in Armenian society included the Social Democrats, the Social Revolutionaries, and the Populists. Only the Dashnaks and the Populists participated in the Armenian government, since the Democrats and Revolutionaries fell outside the pale of Armenian nationalism and favored varying types of relationships with the Soviets. Such contemplated arrangements were then an anathema to most Armenians.

The Armenian republic hobbled along, attempting to deal with its monumental problems within the cramped confines of one of the smallest and most underdeveloped regions of the former Romanov Empire. It was soon recognized by the Armenian leadership that a more adequate mechanism for the protection of the Armenian people was necessary. In 1920 the U.S. government was asked, in view of the sympathetic expression voiced by President Wilson concerning the plight of the Armenians, to assume a mandate over Armenia. In turn, Wilson formally requested congressional approval. Congress, however, refused the president's request to the dismay of the Armenian community and their sympathizers.

The next attempt in the search for national security was getting the Turks to agree to a comprehensive final treaty that would rectify the numerous wrongs committed under the Ottoman administration. It was the Treaty of San Sevres that provided for Turkish recognition of the Armenian republic, having involved the arbitration of the U.S. government in the designation of the final borders to be established between Armenia and Turkey. This treaty, it will be recalled, called for the independence or autonomy of the Hejaz, Kurdistan, Yemen, Egypt, Cyprus, Tripoli, Mesopotamia, Syria, Palestine, and Arabia. Turkey was to be truncated to a fraction of the domains of the former Ottoman Empire. Its finances were to be under Allied control, and its army reduced to a shadow of what it had previously been.

Though the Young Turks had been party to the agreement, the Turkish Nationalists, led by Mustafa Kemal (later Mustafa Kemal Ataturk), refused to recognize the Armenian republic and launched a rebellion against the central Ottoman government for its betrayal, willingly or unwillingly, of the "fatherland" to the foreign occupiers (the Entente powers). The Kemalists began a full insurrection in September 1920, having declared Ankara as the new Turkish capital. Nonetheless, despite the initial successes, Kemal was temporarily routed.

The European powers and the Soviets appeared committed to enforcing the Treaty of Sevres yet, due to betrayal and disinterest, the treaty was doomed to failure. The French, for example, began to secretly negotiate with the Kemalists without informing the British. The Bolsheviks were energetically courting the Turks against the British and the French. Italy was impotent, nor would the United States intervene. Moreover, French, Italian, and Soviet money found its way into Kemalist coffers. By September 1920, the Turks and the Soviets had secretly concluded a deal by which the Soviet Union would relinquish certain parts of Armenia, in return for the incorporation of the Armenian Republic into the Soviet Union and the formation of an alliance with Turkey against the British. The Soviets invaded and occupied Armenia and forced the Armenian government to renounce the Treaty of Sevres to permit the Soviet army free passage to Turkey and to agree to Soviet arbitration of the Armeno/Turkish boundary dispute. On November 29, in the company of emissaries from the Soviet Union, the establishment of a pro-Soviet Armenian Revolutionary Committee was announced. On December 2, 1920, the <u>Dashnak</u> government, hopelessly caught in the Soviet/Turkish pincer, signed an accord with the Soviet Union, abdicated its responsibilities to a pro-Moscow junta, which immediately preceded the demise of independent Armenia and its transformation into the Soviet Armenian Republic. Much of the lands that had formerly been in the free Armenian republic had been ceded to Turkey. It is this status quo that persists to this day.

SOVIET ARMENIA

In the interim, the Soviet Armenian Republic has served as the primary vehicle for Armenian national expression. Despite the truncation of historic Armenia in size, and limitations for independent action, the Soviet Armenian Republic has become the national center of the dispersed Armenian people.

Presently, the Soviet Armenian Republic is, by some accounts, the most developed republic in the Soviet Union. A mountainous country, it is the second smallest republic in the Soviet Union. Over 98 percent of the Soviet Armenians are literate, and the proliferation of cultural and literary institutions is amazing. Armenian culture, while finding expression within the confines of official ideological guidelines, has provided a great resurgence in traditional Armenian folkways. Science, technology, and medicine have been greatly advanced by the research undertaken by Soviet Armenians. Additionally, the Institute for Armenological Studies was founded in 1935 and has constantly produced fine scholars. An impressive Armenian national archive, the Library of Illuminated Manuscripts, has been founded in Soviet Armenia. The Catholicate of Soviet Armenia is a beacon for the Armenian Church worldwide. As in all Soviet republics, there is a strict separation between church and state.

The progress made in cultural, economic, and social developments under the Soviets has been profound. The question, however, is the relationship of the republic to the Armenian people as a whole. Many Armenians are dissatisfied with the degree of self-government Armenia actually exercises under Soviet control. On the one hand, most Armenians now reside in Soviet Armenia, yet the number of Armenians emigrating from the large Armenian diaspora into the Soviet Armenian Republic remains small. Additionally, many Armenians harbor hope that more of historic Armenia can be reclaimed by the Armenian nation, even if this reclamation is to be absorbed by the Armenian republic under Soviet tutelage.

The many frustrations of the Armenian diaspora communities concerning the incorporation of Armenia into the Soviet Union and the continued administration of sizable parts of historic Armenia by Turkey is, however, at least partially countervailed by the existence of one place that the Armenians can call their own. After a century replete with the worst calamities that can be suffered by a people, the Armenians can now look forward to a period of national rejuvenation. The massacres of 1915-16 had almost succeeded in extinguishing hope for any collective Armenian future. National extinguishment, at least, has been eluded.

8

REDEFINING THE MIDDLE EAST:
THE QUESTION OF
SELF-DETERMINATION

The lament in George Bernard Shaw's Man and Superman, which states of humanity that "the cup of our ignominy is full," can aptly be used to describe the world's neglect of the submerged nationalities of the Middle East. The reductionist view of the Middle East that stresses the Arab-Israel conflict to the exclusion of the myriad of issues affecting the region's disenfranchised peoples demonstrates the degree to which our knowledge of world affairs is informed by propaganda.

In the Middle East, the yoke of Ottomanism has been removed, but the equality of peoples in the region has not come about. Nominal independence has been achieved, but liberty remains the perogative of moneyed elites whose fabulous wealth from oil has been bought at the expense of democracy and civil liberties at the grassroots level. The apparent end of colonialist endeavor that we believed to have come about at midcentury continues in the form of an insidious partnership transpiring between the region's ruling elites and multinational petroleum corporations. The West and the Soviet bloc are united in reinforcing the misbegotten rule of the region's governing elites. The profit margins of oil companies and strategic advantage are substituted for principled actions aimed at rectifying the historical wrongs to which the peoples of the Middle East remain subjected.

The premises that dictate the conventional understanding of contemporary Middle Eastern affairs are debunked after the history of the region is examined. A review of Middle Eastern history demands that the following points be recognized when considering Middle East affairs today:

1. The pandemic violence that wracks the Middle East is not attributable to one Arab-Israel conflict, but to a host of confrontations resulting from the political culture of the region.

2. The historical antecedents of this political culture are found in:
   (a) the duration of Ottoman feudalism in the region; (b) the European
   penetration of the region; (c) the deottomanization of the Middle
   East and its replacement by Western colonialism; (d) the substitu-
   tion of Western colonialism by the mandatory system in the post-
   World War I era; and (e) the transfer of overt power from the departing Western mandatory power to indigenous elite power centers.
3. In fundamental respects, the establishment of numerous Middle
   Eastern states came about in conformity with foreign interests
   rather than out of the genuine needs and aspirations of the citizens
   of these nascent states.
4. Foreign intervention in Middle Eastern affairs, though different in
   form from the colonial system used in the region until after World
   War I, is preserved through the relationship maintained by the
   multinational petroleum concerns and their governments with the
   ruling elites of the region; the Eastern bloc operates in a similar
   fashion with respect to the region, although its influence is exercised through the deployment of military advisors and armaments
   at the behest of "friendly" rulers.
5. The prevailing political culture in the Middle East has the following
   parameters: (a) economic and political power is concentrated in the
   hands of numerically small elites whose rise to power, virtually
   without exception, came about through nondemocratic means such
   as coups d'etat; (b) legislation in the states of the Middle East comes
   about by fiat from the ruling elites; (c) all legislative, judicial, and
   military functions are determined by the governing elites with little
   if any consultation with, or recourse by, the citizens; (d) pan-
   Arabic, pan-Islamic, or "revolutionary" legitimizing creeds are
   prosecuted by the elites; (e) the absence of civil liberties and elementary democratic rights is justified by a continuing national state
   of crisis represented by "imperialism and Zionism"; (f) calls for
   the redistribution of power within these states is viewed as "sub-
   version"; and (g) the denial of minority rights, of autonomy for
   submerged ethnicities, and the hegemony of Arabic language and
   culture is an integral part of the region's political culture.

The political culture of the regimes governing the majority of Middle
Eastern states is subordinated to the self-sustaining interests of the
ruling elites, who justify their perpetuation by projecting the view that
they are their nation's "guardians." While the aspects of this political
culture, as described above, may differ depending on transient events
in the region, this mode of government is dominant throughout the
Middle East.

THE STATES AND THE NATIONS

In terms of the ethnonational groups inhabiting the region, the Middle East is manifestly heterogeneous. Such terms as "majority" and "minority" offer little insight into the realities of the region; the Kurds, for example, are a minority when their numbers in Turkey, Syria, Iraq, and Iran are weighed against the total populations of these countries. The Kurds, though, when another point of reference is used, are a preponderant majority in the contiguous swath of territory that has been known throughout history as Kurdistan.

Similarly, the Armenians, now scattered by a vast diaspora, had throughout history been a sovereign nation residing in the country known as Armenia or Haristan, as it is known in Armenian. So, too, the Berbers struggling for national "minority" rights in Algeria actually constitute a majority of that country's inhabitants, as they have for millenia. In view of the autonomy and independence enjoyed throughout history by such groups as the Kurds, Berbers, Azerbiajanis, Baluch, Druze, and Armenians, it is a cruel irony that these groups are now subjugated in the age of national "liberation" by regimes that rule over previously nonexistent nation-states. In a macabre twist of history, these groups, which had exercised dominion over their native lands and developed proud cultures, are now virtually unknown to the outside world. Today these indigenous societies continue in the villages and towns where they have been ensconced for thousands of years. Their lives, though, are now governed by elites that seek to eclipse their identities. Bitterly, these submerged groups have learned during their decades of subjugation that no effort will be spared by their rulers to subvert their survival as unique ethnic groups.

The anamolous status of the Middle Eastern minorities was largely presaged by the international accords that were devised in the aftermath of World War I. In the Treaty of Sevres, for example, which formally ended World War I, conditions were stipulated that called for the independence of Armenia and for Kurdish autonomy. The Treaty of Sevres, however, was superseded by the Treaty of Lausanne, which discarded the principles of national self-determination contained in the Treaty of Sevres. In the transition, international law effectively swept the Armenians from control over their country and permitted Kurdistan to be swallowed up by the nascent states of Iraq, Syria, Turkey, and Iran. These international accords served to wipe away any prospect for authentic emancipation of many Middle Eastern ethnonational groups and paved the way for subsequent suppression of most of these groups by the emergent elites. By so doing, the global powers potentiated the violence that has today become a way of life in the Middle East. Although the formal era of European colonialism in the Middle East ended earlier in this century, in a very real way the legacy of colonialism continues in the Middle East today.

European colonialism began with the demise of feudalism, which brought the advent of mercantilism, from which capitalism derived. The industrial revolution introduced dramatic technological innovations. The new demands made by industrialization on society prompted the captains of industry to seek economic advantages that would propel their productivity beyond that of their competitors. Resources, both material and human, were limited in their own lands. Accordingly, the Europeans sought the advantages of resources abroad through the device of imperialism.

The geographical proximity of the Middle East along with its great wealth of resources held great promise for the European imperialists. Further, the Middle East had been weakened by four centuries of Ottomanism, which had sapped the region of all vitality. The region slumbered, its potential depleted by the vagaries of Ottoman feudalism, and it was ripe for European penetration. The injuries that incurred from European imperialism roused the region from its malaise.

Mehemed Ali, the Arabian who arrived on the shores of Egypt as part of an army loyal to the Turkish sultan but who remained to found an empire of his own in the Middle East, was the first European to push the region toward the modern era. Along with his sons, he tore away the distant appendages claimed by the sultanate and by so doing sowed the seeds that would bring the fall of the Ottoman Empire. Mehemed Ali and his supporters revived the dying spirit of Arabism, firing the imagination of a people that had long been dormant under the weight of the Turkish Empire. The new dynamism that came about in the region further heartened the European powers in their search for new sources of markets and resources.

The centrifugal forces inherent to European capitalism brought imperialism to the Middle East in the nineteenth century. The requisites of imperialism required an expanded communications and transit route to the East that passed through the Middle East. Accordingly, the French built the Suez Canal in an effort to "shorten" the distance between Europe and east Asia. The canal was then acquired by the British and made virtually a part of Europe.

Foreign troops were introduced into the area by the Europeans to protect their colonial assets, and new superstructures, the colonial offices, pressed their imprint on the Middle East. The region's potential was quickly realized by the European powers, and laboring under the demands of imperialism they competed energetically to gain control over as much of the resources in the region as possible.

In Lebanon, the French helped the Christians of the country develop new industries that served to stratify the native population and establish a French bridgehead in the Middle East. In the Sudan and southern Egypt, the British quickly established huge cotton plantations for the purpose of providing the textile factories in England with raw materials. The Germans sought to establish a Berlin-to-Baghdad railroad that would expedite the exploitation of the Middle East's natural resources, including petroleum. They had the foresight to recognize that petroleum's many derivatives would play a critical role in modernization. Therefore, the Germans routed their railroad along petroleum deposits, and by so doing they became the first of the European powers to enter the petroleum era.

DEOTTOMANIZATION AND THE GERRY-MANDERING OF THE REGION

European imperialism acquired different shapes, depending on the power involved. The British employed a "soft" approach toward the Ottomans. Rather than confronting the sultanate in its primary areas of control, the British concentrated their efforts in areas where the sultan's control was weak. By penetrating northern Africa and the Arabian Peninsula, areas that were not critical to the functioning of the Ottoman Empire were incorporated into the British imperialist enterprise.

The French were less gentle. They arrived at ports much closer to the seat of Ottomanism. They realized that the decrepitude that by then had pervaded the empire rendered the sultanate incapable of raising any kind of meaningful resistance to the French colonialist venture, and so they invaded the region without concern for the Ottoman's sovereignty. The Germans, unlike the British and French, sought to reap the fruits of the dying Ottoman Empire not by confronting it, but by coopting it. They dealt directly with the Ottomans, bringing new hope that the empire would be rescued in partnership with German imperialism. Turkey chose to enter the German orbit in the European competition for new sources of materials.

As history subsequently showed, the combined efforts of the Allies exceeded the strength of the Central Powers and their Middle Eastern allies. The great imperialist scramble for the East resulted in an Allied victory. With the European imperial competition behind them, the Allies divided the region among themselves. Negotiations were opened for carving up the region and accords such as the Sykes-Picot Agreement were reached. A new system, the mandatory system, was developed, one that could keep apace of the changing economic and political conditions. However, this neoimperialist system was imposed on the region without the consent of the governed.

Territories in the Middle East were placed under British and French spheres of influence. In these spheres, the Europeans were free to administer the countries and peoples as they wished, a prerogative that was formalized through granting mandatory status to these territories by the League of Nations. The British and French now dealt directly with the indigenous populations of the region, which had grown wrathful after centuries of Ottoman decadence and were increasingly resentful of the aloof arrogance displayed by the Western imperialists in their exploitation of their country's resources.

The same ruthlessness that the French demonstrated toward the Ottomans in the pre-World War I period was also used against the native population in the post war period. However, as a result of such revolts as the Druze rebellion of the early 1920s, new challenges confronted the Europeans in their efforts to govern the region. Although the British ruled their territories more benevolently than the French did, they were not immune from the anti-imperialist fervor that mounted among the indigenous populations. It became clear to the Europeans that their colonialist bid in the Middle East was not open-ended. The Europeans recalculated their needs and realized that political control over the region was not imperative to their concerns. As long as their economic and strategic interests could be preserved, their flags need not fly over Cairo, Baghdad, and Damascus. Therefore, their attention became directed to the development of a new form of rule that lacked the outward features of colonialism but which nonetheless acted in accord with their economic and strategic concerns.

Out of the European spheres of influence arose new nation-states. Whereas the Ottomans had the discretion to hewn their vilayets in accordance with prevailing ethnonational realities, the Europeans did not fetter themselves by such encumbrances. Directing their cartographers to draw with a view toward optimal economic exploitation of the area, entirely new polities came into existence. For example, the country of Iraq was created, uniting together the formerly disparate Ottoman vilayets of Baghdad, Basra, and Mosul. Similarly, out of the desert in the north of the Arabian Peninsula, a new kingdom was established, the Hashemite Kingdom of Jordan. The lands of the Nile were cut into Egypt and the Sudan. The fact that over 500 different ethnic groups resided in the gargantuan land of the Sudan did not deter the British from forging a state there. For British purposes, the intricacies of imperialist economy had made a country out of the highly variegated Sudan. Arabia itself was cut into emirates, new sultanates, and protectorates. European economic and strategic needs, therefore, largely determined the boundaries of a host of new states.

What had been an Ottoman monolith was shattered. Although Turkish hegemony was finally crushed, the fragmentation of the region took place in accord with decisions made in London and Paris as opposed to cohering with indigenous needs. The brief interlude between Ottoman hegemony and the transfer of power to native elites was filled by European mandatory control over the region. In this period, enough groundwork was laid by the imperialists to insure that affairs transpiring in the region would be more in league with European concerns than with domestic ones for many years to come. The region was gerrymandered, and power elites were installed to govern over the misshaped polities. In the cases of many of these states, such as Iraq and Jordan, the new rulers, though native to the Middle East, came from lands distant from the territories they were to rule. This was the case with the Hashemites, who rose out of the Arabian desert to rule over lands that they had barely come to know. This arbitrary development of polities in the Middle East, the author submits, forms the basis for today's pandemic violence in the region.

Overtly, a transfer of power took place between the departing mandatory powers and the power centers that gained control over the region. The process of decolonization began in the early 1920s and continued into the third quarter of this century, when nominal independence was achieved by the states in the region. Even after formal independence, foreign control was preserved over the region by a number of devices. European troops were stationed in large numbers throughout the region, and the Western powers were able to wield considerable influence in the area through the deployment of numerous "advisors" in the region who were attached to various arms of the new governments.

NEOIMPERIALISM AND THE NEW STATES

When the stationing of foreign troops became untenable due to indigenous opposition to neoimperialism, the West withdrew its personnel from the region. In their place, the West was able to maintain its economic interests in the region through close cooperation with the private petroleum companies that had gained concessions for drilling and refining in the Middle East. Up to the present, Western governments protect their interests by guiding their foreign policies largely in line with requests made by private petroleum and other multinational corporations. Given the influence of the multinationals, they are able to play an intermediary role between their governments and that of the Middle Eastern oil producers. This works to the benefit of all concerned parties involved in the "arrangement," which, of course, excludes the masses being governed. The political interests of the oil-exporting country are met through economic and military assistance coming from the Western governments; these governments, in exchange for assured and continuing oil supplies from the Middle East, adjust their foreign policy in favor of the oil-producing states; the petroleum conglomerates, whose chief preoccupation is the flow of oil from the Middle East to the West so that their profit margins can be maintained are assured of these aims by the intergovernmental agreements they facilitate between their host and home governments.

A symbiosis is achieved between the Middle East and the West as a result of trilateral relations between the Mideast oil-producing countries, the Western governments, and the intervening corporations. The ruling elites are able to further consolidate their control over their countries due to the immense wealth they accumulate from their enhanced economic positions. The sale of military weaponry by the West to the states of the Arabian Peninsula is an example of how this symbiosis functions to the advantage of the governing elites and the Western states, whose military-industrial complex flourishes intact.

The Soviet Union and the Eastern bloc have worked in a similar fashion in forging ties with the governments of the Middle East. The Eastern bloc is less in need of foreign oil than of favorable strategic position. The Middle Eastern elites with which the Soviet bloc maintains positive relations reciprocate Soviet support by offering facilities in their countries for use by the Soviet military. In return, the Kremlin provides concrete support to its allies in the region.

The net effect of the assistance received from both the West and the Eastern bloc is the further entrenchment of the ruling elites in the Middle East. The elites become increasingly indispensable to foreign interests that support them materially, and accordingly they rule without the criticism their repressive regimes might otherwise receive from foreign governments. These elites are too dear to Western and Soviet bloc interests to warrant castigation. Consequently, the internal affairs of the Middle Eastern states proceed unscrutinized by most of the outside world. The result of this privileged status has been the continued suppression of submerged ethnonational groups in the Middle East and the systematic deprivation of civil rights for all the citizens of the region.

On the surface, the second half of the twentieth century will be remembered as a time when power was transferred from the former imperialist countries to indigenous, Middle Eastern control. One might point to the establishment of over 20 Arab states, of republican Turkey, and of independent Iran as definitive proof that the cause of liberty in the Middle East was advanced by decolonization. However, what is of importance from the standpoint of self-determination—which the author defines as the right of groups and individuals to govern their socioeconomic, political, and cultural affairs without extended encumbrances—is the conspicuous absence of vehicles by which Kurds, Armenians, Berbers, African Sudanese, Druze, Dhofaris, Baluch, and other ethnonational groups can gain control over their own collective existences. These ethnonational groups are far from having achieved genuine emancipation in the postcolonial era. This can be attributed squarely to the fact that the transfer of power from

the West to indigenous power centers did not produce a distribution
of that power among the region's many ethnonational groups and socioeconomic classes.

Stated somewhat differently, the transfer of power from the imperialists to indigenous power centers did not result in the sharing of
that power among different sectors of Middle Eastern society. What
has come about instead of equitable power distribution is the establishment of new ruling elites who govern over polities that have no basis
for nationhood from the point of view of national cohesiveness. The
rule of the new elites in the Middle East does not derive from national
consensus. Many of the elites came to power in the wake of revolutions
that expelled the colonialist presence from the region. They were part
of a popular movement to rid the region of an external oppressor, but
they did not achieve power through popular mandate. Virtually without
exception, the elites governing today's Middle East were never elected,
nor do they represent a national consensus. These elites seized the
reigns of state through coups d'etat and other forms of power usurpation. They function without democratic sanction, and they govern in
the worst traditions of paternal authoritarianism. These elites, which
are most often comprised of the military, govern according to their
own ideological and/or self-interested agendas. Often the items on
these agendas contradict national priorities.

THE MANIPULATION OF GROUP IDENTITIES

One of the most prevalently used instruments by which these
elites maintain power is the manipulation of group identities and legitimizing creeds. The Algerian leadership, for example, is able to use
its anticolonialist legacy to justify its current rule. It asserts that the
continued centralization of power in the hands of a tightly knit governing clique is justified in the face of continuing external threats in the
form of imperialism and Zionism. These two threats, the Algerian
leadership alleges, pose a danger to Algeria, which is manifested by
the dispossession of the Palestinians and by Israel's continued occupation of lands taken during the 1967 Arab-Israel War. The Algerian
leadership exhorts its citizens to mobilize behind it and to endure the
shortcomings of elite government in view of the dangers emanating
from the West and Israel. Arab unity is the legitimizing creed that is
utilized by the Algerian elite to justify the sacrifices it demands of its
citizenry in the continuing "anti-imperialist" struggle. Algeria, however, is populated by Berbers; it is fraudulent to impose an "Arab"
identity on this predominantly non-Arab people, and one must question
the Algerian elite's motivations in doing so.

The manipulation of group identities by the Algerian establishment does not represent an imperative of state, but rather it pertains to the interests of a self-perpetuating elite. Similarly, the pan-Arab governments of Iraq and Syria compel their non-Arab citizens, such as Kurds, Turcomans, Druze, and ethnic Persians, to fight wars on behalf of "Arabdom" against the "Zionist entity." It is self-evident that the interests of the Iraqi and Syrian citizenries lie more in the attainment of an equitable distribution of national wealth and the achievement of civil liberties and democratic rule rather than in the anti-Israel adventurism of their pan-Arabist leaders.

Since the regimes of the Middle East do not result from popular mandate by and large, the elites seek legitimizing creeds that can serve to unify their citizenry. Most often, the legitimization formulas are of a pan-Arabic, pan-Islamic bent. The fact that many of these countries are inhabited largely by non-Arabs reflects the essence of the problem. By projecting the legitimizing creed of pan-Arabism, the elites of the Middle East are able to preclude power sharing among the various ethnonational groups they govern. The allocation of massive quantities of national resources on such diversionary enterprises as the struggle against Israel offers a justification by which democratic rule and citizen participation in national affairs can be preempted. By fostering the notion that an unabating crisis faces their countries in the form of Israel, the elites offer a rationalization by which their misconduct of government is overlooked. After all, only traitors question governmental authority in times of national crisis. By declaring that Israel presents a continuing national threat, the elites are able to stonewall any internal criticism of their regimes.

THE ARAB-ISRAELI CONFLICT

The Arab-Israel conflict offers the ruling elites of the Moslem Middle East a convenient pretext for engaging in misrule. The Arab elites have successfully introduced the Arab-Israel conflict as the main malaise affecting the region: no United Nations debate takes place concerning the region without some allusion to the conflict. At the "crux" of the hostilities of the Middle East conflict—which is equated with the Arab-Israel conflict to the exclusion of all other issues—is the Palestinian problem, according to Arab apologists. The Palestinians are, indeed, a downtrodden people. They are not, however, the only ethnonational group in the Middle East to be suppressed, and given the overwhelming amount of attention paid by the Arab regimes to the problem, one is compelled to question the motivations of the elites in subordinating all other regional issues to the Palestinian problem.

When analyzing the championship of the Palestinian campaign

on the part of the Arab elites, there appears to be a considerable
schism between words and deeds. The Hashemite Kingdom of Jordan,
for example, professes pious fidelity to Palestinian national rights.
Yet, during "Black September" in 1970, King Hussein unleashed the
full force of his Bedouin army against the Palestinians in his country.
Similarly, Saudi Arabia, which is a major extoller of Palestinian self-
determination and has expended millions of dollars to finance terrorist
attacks in the name of Palestinianism, has refused to grant citizenship
to the Palestinians living within its borders. Some Palestinians may
have been born and bred in Saudi Arabia; indeed, they may never have
cast eyes on another land. Nonetheless, citizenship is not accorded to
such individuals. Surely, granting citizenship to a Palestinian is not
incompatible with efforts to attain a Palestinian state. In such a con-
text, serious suspicions concerning the true significance of Palestinianism to the Saudi elite naturally arise.

Saudi Arabia projects itself to be an unwavering proponent of
Palestinian self-determination. There are, though, other Arab regimes
whose militancy on the Palestinian question surpasses even that of
Saudi Arabia. Syria and Iraq, for example, are leaders of the Arab
Rejectionist and Steadfastness Front. These states contend that there
can be no recognition, no negotiations, and no peace with Israel. The
ruling elites at the helm of these states demand, minimally, the return by Israel of all lands taken during the 1967 Arab-Israel War and
the establishment on these lands of a Palestinian state. Syrian President Assad claims to have the interests of the Palestinians so close
to heart that his government would "never recognize Israel, not even
if the PLO did so." This strident statement is paradoxical when con-
trasted to Syria's frequent statements that Palestine is part of "historic Syria." If Palestine is part of Syria, why does the Syrian elite
clamor so for a Palestinian entity? Why does it not enter negotiations
with Israel for the return of lands that they believe to be rightly theirs?
The Palestinians, however, do not consider themselves to be "southern Syrians," and Assad's attempts to manipulate Palestinian identity
is indicative of territorial ambitions more than of a principled concern
for the Palestinians.

There is a strange kind of logic to Iraq's advocacy of a Palestinian state. It is by a perverse twist of reason that the Iraqis would
exert such strenuous efforts on behalf of the Palestinians while they
deploy their military in anti-insurgency attacks of near genocidal proportions in Iraqi Kurdistan. Not only have the Iraqis failed to remedy
the status of Kurds in that country, but they have worsened it immeasurably since the pan-Arabist Baath party took control of the country
in the early 1960s. Nevertheless, the Iraqi representatives at the
United Nations frequently cite the principle of self-determination and
national liberation with respect to the Palestinians, despite the fact

that Iraq wantonly disregards these principles with respect to its own national minority problems.

Syria and Iraq's colleagues in the Arab Rejectionist and Steadfastness Front include the leaders of Libya and Algeria, both of which pride themselves in their "rejectionist" policies toward Israel. They reject the notion of achieving peace with Israel, since they believe that Israel has usurped Arab lands and that Israel is exclusively responsible for the Palestinian problem. Despite their adamant calls for Palestinian national rights, both Algeria and Libya suppress their large Berber populations through forced Arabization. Algeria acts to crush all protests regarding that government's attempts to stifle Berber language and folk culture in outlying areas of the country. Libya's leader, Colonel Muammar Qadaffi, has gone so far as to say that there is no such phenomenon as the Berbers: he has sought to foist a pariah status on the Berbers by arguing that their existence is a product of "colonialist culture." Obviously, this assertion runs counter to Berber self-perception, but it is through denial and imposed acculturation that the Libyan leader hopes to solve the Berber question in his country. Against this backdrop, it is difficult to take these leaders' stated commitments to Palestinian self-determination seriously when these very same elites are responsible for denying cultural autonomy to large ethnonational groups within their own countries.

In addition to a concern for Palestinian rights that rings hollow, the member-states of the Arab Rejectionist and Steadfastness Front and other Middle Eastern elite groups share other common features of government. All of the states are governed by numerically small elites, such as the minority Alawite regime of Syria's President Assad, the Revolutionary Command Council of Libya's Colonel Qadaffi, or the feudal family oligarchies of the Arabian Peninsula such as Bahrain's al-Khalifa elite. These regimes enforce internal policies that are most repressive: indeed, the cost for dissension is often execution. These states are protected against internal opposition by omnipresent security forces that scrutinize every aspect of public life and often personal life as well. As a rule, public policy is handed down from these elites by fiat. Once promulgated, policies are rarely rescinded.

THE LIMITS OF CITIZEN PARTICIPATION

There is little if any public participation in the policy-making process, and where constituencies are represented by elected officials—which is the case in only a few of the states under discussion—the input of these elected representatives seldom receives any consideration from the elites. Almost without exception, no instrument of government protects the civil liberties of the private citizen. Administrative detention, such as those that took place in the months just prior to the assassination of Egyptian President Anwar Sadat, are commonplace and recourse to the due process of law is rarely a viable alternative. The judiciary and legislative functions of government are, for the most part, indistinguishable from the executive branch.

All aspects of public life, including education, the media, and culture, are tightly controlled by the government. Islam is the state religion of all Middle Eastern states, with the exclusion, of course, of Israel and, at least formally, of Lebanon and Turkey.

In sum, public life in the Middle East is authoritarian in character. The elites render law, and accordingly they are above any check on their administration. Government is held by regimes that retain absolute power. At best, in countries such as the Sudan where government is in the hands of a relatively benevolent regime, the nature of government is paternalistic. In other states, such as Syria, Iraq, and Libya, government is employed with utter disregard for the rights of the individual or, for that matter, of the nation.

The states of the Middle East are not only authoritarian with respect to internal government, but together these regimes impose a totalitarian character on the region as a whole. Woefully little pluralism is practiced in matters pertaining to the free exchange of ideas, religious belief, culture, or group identity. Many observers of the Middle East regard the region as being largely an Arab domain. However, this attests more to the strength of the indigenous elites in manipulating group identity than to the actual makeup of society in the region. Although the countries of the Maghreb are member-states of the League of Arab States, the designation of these predominantly Berber societies as being "Arab" countries is ludicrous. To characterize Mauritania as being an "Arab" state is absurd for anyone whose knowledge of that country extends at least as far as the meaning of its name, which translates into "the land of the Moors." Somalia, whose Hamatic population, again as its name denotes, is constituted by the unique Somali people, can be construed as being an Arab country only with reference to the language used by its leaders.

If the Sudan is to be regarded as an Arab country, what is to be the status of the millions of non-Arab Africans who inhabit the south of that country? To declare that Iraq is an Arab country is to add insult to the many injuries endured by that country's Kurds, Turcomans, and ethnic Persians. Similarly, the Kurds, Druze, and other minority groups of Baathist Syria face discrimination on the basis of the officially Arab character of their state. The monolithic identity of the region in terms of the Arab identity of its elites belies any claim to pluralistic government that these regimes may make. Manifestly, ethnic hegemony in favor of elites asserting Arab identity mitigates any possibility of peaceful coexistence between the region's many ethnonational groups. No Middle East government promotes inter-group parity, and multinational states such as Iraq and Iran do not admit any measure of power sharing among different ethnic, linguistic, and religious groups.

The limits of Arab identity are stretched to absurdity by the spectacle of elites claiming Arab identity in countries for their patently non-Arab societies. Arab designation appears to have more to do with power politics in the region than with the actual composition of society in the Middle East. Arabism has become a racialist prerogative of Middle Eastern elites who reject the concept of power sharing between different ethnonational groups in the region. Pan-Arabism posits "Arab" identity and solidarity in the face of supposed external threats, such as Israel. In reality, such solidarity is exhorted by elites only when their security is endangered. Most often the security of these elites does not coincide with that of their nation as a whole.

In view of the totalitarian character of Mideast government today, whereby Arab identity is projected over a broad sweep of land without regard to the millions of non-Arabs residing there, a number of questions concerning the region arises. For example, is the threat represented by Israel a danger to the peoples of the Middle East or, more accurately, is it a danger only to the elites that govern the region? Although one might point to the establishment of Israel as being a factor in the statelessness of the Palestinians, one has to resort to political acrobatics to explain how Israel is a danger to the fellah in Tunisia or Iraq. Israel is often described as disrupting the unity of the Arab world, which is said to extend from "the Atlantic and Mediterranean to the Tigris and Eupherates." But this great expanse of territory does not consist of a single nation; it is a highly heterogeneous community of ethnic, linguistic, and religious groups, many of which have no relation whatsoever to the Arab legacy. The underlying question concerns the reasons that Arab identity is imposed on the region. What motivates the ruling elites of the region to profess such a monolithic identity?

TOTALITARIANISM IN THE MIDEAST TODAY

The reasons for totalitarianism in the Middle East today rest on the following premises: If the Middle East is discovered to be far less homogeneous than is widely presumed, Israel is not the foreign interloper it is claimed to be by its Arab detractors. Further, if the elites of the region were to permit the existence of Israel as a state representing the needs and aspirations of a people that from the regional point of view is a minority, what is to prevent the other ethnonational groups from seeking national minority rights, free cultural expression and, ultimately, statehood in those areas where they constitute a majority?

The elites of the Middle East are forced by their own inadequacies to project a unified ethnic composition, if they are not to be castigated for denying self-determination to those groups that they suppress. If the notion of power sharing were to be legitimized on the regional level between ethnonational groups, what impediment lies in the way of power sharing on the national level through internal liberalization? If such reform were achieved, what would sustain the legitimacy of the ruling elites? The answer is, simply, that nothing supports these elites if power sharing is introduced on any level in the Middle East. The virtual dictatorships maintained by the elites of the Middle East would unravel with either the admissibility of power sharing between ethnic groups or the lessening of state power of the regimes governing the Middle East.

Therefore, the danger posed by Israel to the ruling elites of the Middle East does not derive from any tangible fault of that nation. Rather, the danger is a symbolic one, since Israel represents the possibility of self-determination for the region's non-Arab population. The only way by which Israel can possibly be accused of being a threat to the Middle East lies in the equation of national interests within the states of the region with the self-interested concerns of the governing elites. To state such an equation, to identify the national interests of the states in the Middle East with those of the elites is to claim that the peoples of the region have an interest in patriarchy, authoritarianism, repressive internal policies, and the concentration of political and economic power in the hands of governing cliques.

The illegitimacy of the regimes of the Moslem Middle East is not cited to whitewash Israel's wrongdoings; nor is it to claim that Palestiniansim has no justification. Insofar as Palestinianism represents the authentic need of a stateless people, the cause of Palestinian nationalism is fully justified. Tragically, the view of Palestinianism as having as its sine qua non the elimination of Israel is strongly propagated by the Arab elites. These elites maintain that Zionism and Palestinianism are mutually exclusive. This perspective, however, has far more to do with the politics of survival for the ruling elites of the Middle East than with the actual nature of Palestinianism and Zionism.

Numerous Israeli public figures, especially those on the political left, have explicitly stated that an independent Israel and Palestine can coexist under conditions of mutual recognition of each other's needs and security. Further, a number of Palestinian intellectuals have also intimated this view. Under a two-state solution to the problem, the land claimed by both the Jews and the Palestinians can be shared along with the Israeli-held territories captured in the 1967 Arab-Israel War. The possibility of a two-state solution has been discussed since the 1967 war, yet no Arab public figures with the exception of Egypt's leaders have recognized the potential of this proposal. If the Arab elites are so anxious to solve the Palestinian problem why have they refused to entertain programs that would lead to Palestinian self-determination evolving from a two-state solution to the problem? The answer is to be found in the threat to self-perpetuation of the region's elites for whom the doctrine of self-determination applied to national coexistence in the region is an anathema. Self-determination implies power sharing, which contravenes the absolute control by which the region's ruling elites sustain their rule.

THE DANGER REPRESENTED BY ISRAEL

Although Israel's continued existence and a future Palestinian state are not inherently incompatible, both parties to this conflict repeatedly subvert the possibility of this arrangement. Israeli leaders, especially those of the ruling Likud coalition, persist in propagating the view that the Palestinians do not comprise a people distinct from the neighboring Arab nations. Many Israelis view Palestinianism as consisting of only one movement, that which entertains the belief that Israel must be eliminated to meet the demands of Palestinian nationhood. Given the frequent signals emanating from the Arab world that Palestiniansim does indeed call for the dismantlement of Israel, these Israeli decision makers are not entirely without justification with respect to their apprehensions. Additionally, the Palestine Liberation Organization's ties to Arab elites in the Middle East and their demonstrable intolerance for those voices within the Palestinian community that call for a two-state solution to the problem serve, along with the PLO's terror tactics, to discredit the legitimacy of Palestiniansim in the eyes of the Israeli public.

For its part, Israel's discriminatory policies toward its Arab citizens further widen the schism between Jews and Arabs in the Mideast. Jerusalem must act to accord equal rights to both its Arab and Jewish citizens in all areas of society. To do otherwise places Israel's democracy in danger in addition to the moral damage incurred.

Israel's continued occupation of the West Bank and Gaza Strip denies self-determination to the Palestinians and thus furthers the goals of both Arab and Jewish extremists. Such actions as indiscriminate, punitive bombings of Palestinian installations in Lebanon or the closure of West Bank universities and newspapers do not advance the possibility of Jewish-Palestinian rapprochement. While Israel is fully entitled to security within defensible borders, many of the Likud's

policies extend beyond security needs. Further, they erode the credi-
bility of the few Palestinian elements that seek an accommodation with
Israel. These Palestinians, must function in a decidedly closed, in-
tolerant political culture in which they are a minute and isolated minority. Israel's role with respect to these Palestinian peace activisits
should be the nurturing of a political climate that corroborates the
claims made by these Palestinians, namely, that Israel is a willing
partner in seeking ways to arrive at Palestinian-Jewish coexistence.

While Israeli decision makers should signal a readiness to recognize a two-state solution to the Palestinian problem, the Palestinian
peace camp must expand its numbers to overcome the belligerent nature of the PLO today. The PLO is beset by internal divisions, internal power conflicts, and a virtual surrender to the Arab elites that
control the organization's purse strings. It is conceivable that all the
goodwill in the world will not bring the Palestinian problem to a resolution until the all-pervasive problem of elitist government in the Middle East—that repressive system that subjugates the submerged nationalities of the region—is excised at its roots. Although the Arab
elites profess a concern for Palestinian self-determination, it is du-
bious that such self-determination will come about until the doctrine
of self-rule, free cultural expression, and political and economic
democracy are consistently applied to all the peoples of the Middle
East. Were the ruling Arab elites to agree to the widespread application of such principles they would, in effect, presage their own demise.

The resolution of the Palestinian problem, the achievement by
Israel of security and peaceful coexistence with the peoples surrounding it, and the emancipation of the submerged nationalities of the Middle East await the same conditions for fruition. The Middle East must
be redefined so that elite interests and the identities they manipulate
are replaced by a realistic view of the region. The Middle East is not
the homogeneous monolith it is portrayed as being. It is not a region
beset by only one issue, the Palestinian problem, to the exclusion of
all other matters. National interests should no longer be confused
with the survival of particular elites.

The Middle East is a region that is rich in cultural diversity.
Its inherent dynamism cannot be suppressed by a system of elitist
rule without producing constant violence. To expect the submerged
ethnonational groups of the region to surrender their group identities
in the interest of elite government is far more than can be expected
of any social group. Additionally, to expect that the indigenous populations of the region, both Arab and non-Arab, will continue compla-
cently as elites misgovern their countries is to be naive about the
ultimate consequences of repression. The Middle East must be treated
in accord with its underlying realities, and not on the basis of the par-
ticularistic ideologies of self-appointed rulers.

The redefinition of the Middle East requires a novel approach to the region. In examining the conditions that act to suppress minority groups and that repress all nonelite citizens within the Moslem Middle East, it is necessary to find a political solution conducive to the socioeconomic and cultural needs of the populace. What the people of the Middle East require is the opportunity to freely exercise control over their collective and personal lives without encumbrances such as authoritarian, elitist rule, and racialist totalitarianism. The struggle to conquer the impoverishment of the region cannot be found in the policies of unrepresentative regimes whose interests are predominantly the perpetuation of their misbegotten rule. The call for reform in the region does not constitute a summons to return to the colonialism of the past; nor is it an invitation to foreign interests to intervene anew in the affairs of the region. The redefinition of the Middle East demands self-rule by and for its citizenry.

SELECTED BIBLIOGRAPHY

BOOKS

AlRoy, Gil Carl. Behind the Middle East Conflict. New York: Putnam's Sons, 1975.

Amir, Shimeon. Israel's Development Cooperation with Africa, Asia, and Latin America. New York: Praeger, 1974.

Antonious, George. The Arab Awakening. New York: Paragon, 1979.

Armenia. Moscow: Novosti Press Agency, 1967.

Arnson, Cynthia, Stephen Daggett, and Michael Klare. Crisis In Iran. Washington, D.C.: Institute for Policy Study, n.d.

Arrighi, Giovanni, and John S. Saul. Essays on the Political Economy of Africa. New York: Monthly Review, 1973.

Azerbaijan. Moscow: Novosti Press Agency, 1972.

Bairoch, Paul. The Economic Development of the Third World Since 1900. Berkeley: University of California Press, 1975.

Barbour, K. M. The Republic of the Sudan. London: University of London, 1961.

Barnes, Leonard. Africa in Eclipse. New York: St. Martin's Press, 1971.

Barnet, Richard, and Ronald E. Muller. Global Reach. New York: Simon and Schuster, 1974.

Baulin, Jacques. The Arab Role in Africa. London: Penguin, 1962.

Bechtold, Peter K. Politics in the Sudan. New York: Praeger, 1976.

Bertelson, Judy S., ed. Nonstate Nations in International Politics. New York: Praeger, 1977.

Beshir, Mohamed Omer. The Southern Sudan: Background to Conflict. New York: Praeger, 1968.

Brecher, Michael. Decisions in Israel's Foreign Policy. New Haven: Yale University Press, 1975.

Carmichael, Joel. The Shaping of the Arabs. New York: Macmillan, 1967.

Chaliand, Gerrard, ed. People without a Country: The Kurds and Kurdistan. London: Zed Press, 1980.

Chubin, Shahram, and Sepehr Zabih. The Foreign Relations of Iran. Berkeley: University of California Press, 1974.

Cohen, Aharon. Israel and the Arab World. New York: Funk & Wagnalls, 1970.

Cohen, Mark J., and Lorna Hahn. Morocco: Old Land, New Nation. New York: Praeger, 1966.

Cohen, Saul B. Geography and Politics in a World Divided. New York: Oxford University Press, 1975.

Curtis, Michael, ed. Religion and Politics in the Middle East. Boulder, Colo.: Westview Press, 1981.

Davidson, Basil. A History of West Africa. Garden City, N.Y.: Anchor, 1966.

Davison, Roderic H. Turkey. Englewood Cliffs, N.J.: Prentice-Hall, 1968.

Diocese of the Armenian Church of America. Martyrdom and Rebirth. New York: Lydian Press, 1965.

Draper, Theadore. Israel and World Politics. New York: Viking Press, 1968.

Edmonds, I. G. Allah's Oil. Knoxville: Thomas Nelson, 1977.

El-Asmar, Fouzi. To Be an Arab in Israel. London: Francis Pinter, 1975.

Emmanuel, Arghri. Unequal Exchange. New York: Monthly Review, 1972.

Eprile, Cecil. War and Peace in the Sudan, 1955-1972. London: David and Charles, n.d.

Freedman, Robert O. Soviet Policy toward the Middle East since 1970. New York: Praeger, 1975.

Gal, Allon. Socialist Zionism. Cambridge, Mass.: Schenkman, 1973.

Gathone-Hardy, G. M. The Fourteen Points and the Treaty of Versailles. London: Oxford University Press, 1939.

Gellner, Ernest, and Charles Micaud, eds. Arabs and Berbers. Lexington, Mass.: D.C. Heath, 1972.

Gibb, H. A. R. Mohammedanism. London: Oxford University Press, 1952.

Gilbert, Martin. Atlas of the Arab-Israel Conflict. New York: Macmillan, 1974.

Girvan, Norman. Corporate Imperialism: Conflict and Expropriation. Monthly Review Press, 1976.

Glubb, John. A Short History of the Arab Peoples. New York: Stein and Day, 1969.

Gutkind, Peter, and Peter Waterman. African Social Studies: A Radical Reader. New York: Monthly Review Press, 1971.

Halpern, Ben. The Idea of the Jewish State. Cambridge, Mass.: Harvard University Press, 1969.

Harrison, Selig. In Afghanistan's Shadow: Baluch Nationalism and Soviet Temptations. New York: Carnegie Endowment for International Peace, 1981.

Hartunian, Vartan. Neither to Laugh nor to Weep. Boston: Beacon Press, 1968.

Hertzberg, Arthur. The Zionist Idea. New York: Atheneum, 1959.

Hitti, Philip K. The Arabs. Princeton, N.J.: Princeton University Press, 1949.

Hodgkin, Thomas. Nationalism in Colonial Africa. New York: New York University Press, 1957.

Houranian, Richard G. The Republic of Armenia. Berkeley: University of California Press, 1971.

Hudson, Michael C. Arab Politics: The Search for Legitimacy. New Haven: Yale University Press, 1977.

Hurewitz, J. C. Middle East Politics: The Military Dimension. New York: Praeger, 1969.

Hussaini, Hatem, and Fathalla El-Boghdady, eds. The Palestinians: Selected Essays. Washington, D.C.: Palestine Information Office, n.d.

Ismael, Tareq Y., ed. The Middle East in World Politics. Syracuse, N.Y.: Syracuse University Press, 1974.

Issawi, Charles. The Economic History of the Middle East, 1800–1914. Chicago: University of Chicago Press, 1966.

Ivy, Jean. The Kurds. Jerusalem: Women's International League for Peace and Freedom, Israel Section, n.d.

Jalée, Pierre. The Third World in World Economy. New York: Monthly Review Press, 1969.

Jiryis, Sabri. The Arabs in Israel. New York: Monthly Review Press, 1976.

Kahn, Margaret. Children of the Jinn. New York: Worldview, 1980.

Katz, Samuel. Battleground: Fact and Fantasy in Palestine. New York: Bantam, 1973.

Kedourie, Elie, ed. Nationalism in Asia and Africa. New York: New American Library, 1970.

Kerr, Malcolm. The Arab Cold War. London: Oxford University Press, 1965.

____. The Middle East Conflict. New York: Foreign Policy Association, 1968.

Khadduri, Majid. The Arab-Israeli Impasse. Washington, D.C.: Robert B. Lure, 1968.

_____. Political Trends in the Arab World. Baltimore: Johns Hopkins University Press, 1970.

Kimche, Jon. The Second Arab Awakening. New York: Holt, Rinehart, and Winston, 1970.

Knapp, William. Tunisia. New York: Walker, 1970.

Krammer, Arnold. The Forgotten Friendship: Israel and the Soviet Bloc 1947-53. Urbana: University of Illinois Press, 1974.

Kurdish Democratic Party. On the Kurdish Question at the United Nations. New York: Kurdish Democratic Party, Information Department, 1974.

Landau, Julian J. Israel and the Arabs. Jerusalem: Israel Communications, 1971.

Lanne, Peter. Armenia, The First Genocide of the XX Century. Munich, West Germany: Institute for Armenian Studies, 1977.

Laqueur, Walter. The Israel-Arab Reader. New York: Bantam, 1969.

_____. A History of Zionism. New York: Holt, Rinehart, and Winston, 1972.

_____. Confrontation: The Middle East and World Politics. New York: Bantam, 1974.

Laroui, Abdallah. The Crisis of the Arab Intellectual. London: University of California Press, 1974.

Lenczowski, George. The Middle East in World Affairs. Ithaca, N.Y.: Cornell University Press, 1980.

Magdoff, Harry. The Age of Imperialism. New York: Monthly Review Press, 1969.

Mahgoub, Mohamed Ahmed. Democracy on Trial: Reflections on Arab and African Politics. London: Andre Deutsch, 1974.

Malone, Joseph J. The Arab Lands in Western Asia. Englewood Cliffs, N.J.: Prentice-Hall, 1973.

Manandian, Hacob. A Brief Survey of the History of Ancient Armenia. New York: Diocese of the Armenian Church of America, 1975.

Matheson, Sylvia A. The Tigers of Baluchistan. London: Cox and
    Wyman, 1967.

Memmi, Albert. The Colonizer and the Colonized. Boston: Beacon
    Press, 1967.

_____. Jews and Arabs. Chicago: J. Philip O'Hara, 1975.

Minasian, Rouben Der. Armenian Freedom Fighters: The Memoirs
    of Rouben Der Minasian. Translated by James G. Mandalian.
    Boston: n.p., 1963.

Missakian, J. A Searchlight on the Armenian Question. Boston:
    American Committee for the Independence of Armenia, 1950.

Montagne, Robert. The Berbers. London: Frank Cass, 1973.

Morgenthau, Henry. Ambassador Morgenthau's Story. Phandome,
    N.Y.: New Age, 1919.

Nelson, Harold D., ed. Algeria: A Country Study. Washington, D.C.:
    American University, Foreign Area Studies, 1978.

_____, ed. Morocco: A Country Study. Washington, D.C.: American
    University, Foreign Area Studies, 1978.

_____, ed. Libya: A Country Study. Washington, D.C.: American Uni-
    versity, Foreign Area Studies, 1979.

O'Ballance, Edgar. The Kurdish Revolt, 1961-1970. Hamden, Conn.:
    Anchon Books by Shoestring Press, 1973.

Ozbudun, Ergun. Social Change and Political Participation in Turkey.
    Princeton: Princeton University Press, 1976.

Pehrson, Robert N. The Social Organization of the Mari Baluch.
    Chicago: Aldine, 1966.

Pelt, Adrian. Libyan Independence and the United Nations. New Haven:
    Yale University Press, 1970.

Quandt, William B., Faud Jabber, and Ann Mosely Lesch. The Poli-
    tics of Palestinian Nationalism. Berkeley: University of Cali-
    fornia Press, 1973.

Ramazani, Rouhollah. Iran's Foreign Policy, 1941–1973. Charlottes-
ville: University Press of Virginia, 1975.

Rhodes, Robert I., ed. Imperialism and Underdevelopment. New
York: Monthly Review Press, 1970.

Ronen, Dov. The Quest for Self-Determination. New Haven: Yale
University Press, 1979.

Sachar, Howard M. Egypt and Israel. New York: Richard Marek,
1981.

Said, Edward W. The Question of Palestine. New York: Times Books,
1979.

Sarkisian, E. K., and R. G. Sahakian. Vital Issues in Modern Armenian History. Translated by E. B. Charakian. n.p.: Library
of Armenian Studies, 1965.

Segal, Ronald. Political Africa. London: Stevens and Sons, 1961.

Shahram, Chubin, and Sepher Zabih. The Foreign Relations of Iran.
Berkeley: University of California Press, 1975.

Sharabi, Hisham. Palestine and Israel. New York: Pegasus, 1969.

Sherbiny, Naiem A., and Mark A. Tessler, eds. Arab Oil. New
York: Praeger, 1976.

Shwadran, Benjamin. The Middle East Oil and the Great Powers.
New York: Praeger, 1955.

Sinai, Anne, and Allen Pollack, eds. The Syrian Arab Republic. New
York: American Academic Association for Peace in the Middle
East, 1976.

Sobel, Lester A. Peace-Making in the Middle East. New York: Facts
on File, 1980.

Stork, Joe. Middle East Oil and the Energy Crisis. New York:
Monthly Review Press, 1975.

Sweezy, Paul M. The Theory of Capitalist Development. New York:
Monthly Review Press, 1968.

Sykes, Christopher. Crossroads to Israel 1917-1948. Bloomington: Indiana University Press, 1973.

Tanzer, Michael. The Race for Resources. New York: Monthly Review Press, 1980.

____. The Political Economy of International Oil and the Underdeveloped Countries. New York: Monthly Review Press, n.d.

Toynbee, Arnold J. Armenian Atrocities: The Murder of a Nation. London: Hodder and Stoughton, 1915.

Toynbee, Arnold J., and Kenneth P. Kirkwood. Turkey. New York: Charles Scribner's Sons, 1927.

Vanly, Ismet Cherrif. The Kurdish Problem in Syria. Lausanne: Committee for the Defense of the Kurdish People's Rights, 1968.

Varjabedian, S. H. The Armenians. Chicago: n.p., 1977.

Walinsky, Louis J., ed. The Implications of Israel-Arab Peace for World Jewry. New York: World Jewish Congress, 1981.

Whitaker, Ben. The Fourth World. New York: Schocken, 1973.

Yale, William. The Near East. Ann Arbor: University of Michigan Press, 1958.

ARTICLES

Akinsanya, Adeoye. "The Afro-Arab Alliance: Dream or Reality." African Affairs 75 (October 1976).

Amnesty International, U.S.A. "Syria." Matchbox, November 1981.

____. "Republic of Yemen." Matchbox, November 1981.

Azad, Shahrzad. "Workers' and Peasants' Councils in Iran." Monthly Review 32

Ball, Robert. "The Unseemly Squabble over Iran's Assets." Fortune, January 28, 1980, p. 60.

Bennigsen, Alexandre. "Islam in the Soviet Union." Soviet Jewish Affairs 9 (1979).

Braun, Frank H. "Morocco: Anatomy of a Palace Revolution that Failed." International Journal of Middle East Studies 9 (1978): 63–72.

Brown, L. Carl. "The United States and the Maghrib." Middle East Journal 30 (1976): 273–91.

Colie, Stuart E. "A Perspective on the Shiites and the Lebanese Tragedy." Middle East Review 9 (Fall 1976).

Dekmejian, R. Hrair. "The Armenians: History, Consciousness and the Middle East Dispersion." Middle East Review 9 (Fall 1976).

Economist (London). "The Coming of an Obdurate Messiah." February 3, 1979, p. 37.

Eliot Jr., Theodore L. "Afghanistan: Fact and Fiction." Wall Street Journal, January 9, 1980.

Feili, Omran Yahya, and Arlene R. Fromchuck. "The Kurdish Struggle for Independence." Middle East Review 9 (Fall 1976).

Friedman, Robert. "Report From Beirut: I Know Fatah. They're Bourgeois Swine." Present Tense, Autumn 1981, p. 15.

Goering, Curt. "The Bahais of Iran." Matchbox (Amnesty International, U.S.A.), November 1981, p. 1.

Gruen, George. "Schizophrenic Turkey." Present Tense, Autumn 1981, p. 47.

Halliday, Fred. "Hardliners Have the Upper Hand in Iran's New Cabinet." In These Times, September 17–23, 1980, p. 7.

_____. "Exiles Scheme Against Imam." In These Times, July 16–29, 1980.

Hempstone, Smith. "Khomeini's 'Feast of Blood.'" New Republic 181 (September 22, 1979): 18.

Hirszowicz, L. "The Afghan Crisis in the Soviet Media." Research Report, Institute for Jewish Affairs (London), no. 1, February 1980.

Hourani, A. "Decline of the West in the Middle East." International Affairs 29 (January–April 1953): 156–83.

International League for Human Rights. "Iraq: Persecution of Kurds."
Annual Report, International League for Human Rights (New
York), 1976-77.

Internet Reporter. "The Repression of Kurds in Turkey." Human
Rights Internet Reporter, 6 (May-June 1981): 642.

Jordan, Robert Paul. "Turkey: Crossfire at an Ancient Crossroads."
National Geographic, July 1977.

Jordan, Samos A. "The Mideast Falls Apart." Washington Star,
December 9, 1979, "Commentary" page.

Kimche, Jon. "Selling Out the Kurds." New Republic 172 (April 19,
1975): 19.

Kwitny, Jonathan. "Afghan Communists Battle Poverty, Poor Hygiene,
Entrenched Attitudes." Wall Street Journal, February 6, 1980,
p. 6.

_____. "The Baluch Buffer." Wall Street Journal.

Landau, David. "Eliav Reveals Israel Aided Kurds." Jewish Tele-
graphic Agency Daily Bulletin, May 14, 1978.

Lavrencic, Karl. "UN Aids the Sudan Warriors Build Peace." Gemini
News Service, n.d.

Lerman, Tony. "Islam's Bid for International Political Influence."
Research Report, Institute for Jewish Affairs (London), no.
19, December 1980.

Lippman, W. Thomas. "Egypt's Christian Minority." Middle East
Review 9 (Fall 1976).

Mercer, John. "The Cycle of Invasion and Unification in the Western
Sahara." African Affairs 75 (October 1976).

Middle-East Intelligence Survey. "Iraq: Saddam Husayn Sets Up
a Parliament." 8 (June 16-30, 1979).

Mkape, Ben. "Sudan: A Microcosm of Africa." Times (Dar al-Salaam,
Tanzania), March 2, 1974.

Morrison, Godfrey. "Business Optimism Rekindled as Capital Flows
Back." Times (London), March 25, 1975.

Murray, Andrew. "The Kurdish Struggle." Patterns of Prejudice (London) 9 (July–August 1975).

Naamani, Israel T. "The Kurds in Iraq." Jewish Frontier, July–August 1968.

Oren, Stephen. "The Assyrians of the Middle East." Middle East Review 9 (Fall 1976).

Organisation of Communist Unity. "Kurdistan: Resistance and Further Prospects." Raha'i no. 2 (Summer–Spring 1981).

Petkovic, Ranko. "The History of Non–Alignment." Review (Belgrade, Yugoslav Monthly Review), April–May 1979.

Reed, III, Stanley. "Dateline Syria: Fin De Regime?" Foreign Policy no. 39 (Summer 1980).

Rejwan, Nessim. "The Kurds: Khomeini's Hidden Time Bomb." Hadassah, April 1980, p. 20.

Salibi, Kamal. "The Lebanese Identity." Middle East Review 9 (Fall 1976).

Sinai, Joshua. "Ethnic and Religious Minorities in Egypt, Iraq, Jordan, Lebanon and Syria: A Table." Middle East Review 9 (Fall 1976).

Springborg, Robert. "New Patterns of Agrarian Reform in the Middle East and North Africa." Middle East Journal 31 (Spring 1977): 127-42.

Viorst, Milton. "Israel's Game in Lebanon." The Nation, October 10, 1981, p. 3341.

Waure, Angelo D. "Southern Sudan's Needs Are Vast after 17 Year War." Gemini News Service, November 22, 1974.

Woffall, John. "Three Men Give Hope to the South Sudan." Gemini News Service, November 25, 1975.

Woodson Jr., LeRoy. "We Who Face Death." National Geographic 147 (March 1975).

Young, John. "Sudan: Can a Bridge Built on Good Intentions Stand the Strain?" Times (London), March 25, 1975.

PERIODICALS

Christian Science Monitor.

Jerusalem Post.

New York Times.

Summary of World Broadcasts, Monitoring Service, British Broadcasting Company.

Washington Post.

INDEX

ABOUT THE AUTHOR

Yosef Gotlieb is a writer, lecturer, and editor specializing in Middle East and Third World affairs.

The author's work has appeared in such periodicals as The New York Times, The Los Angeles Times, USA Today, and In These Times. His chapter, "Sectarianism and the Iraqi State," appears in Michael Curtis's (ed.) Religion and Politics in the Middle East (Boulder, Colo.: Westview Press, 1981).

Mr. Gotlieb has served as a consultant to public policy organizations, and he directed the World Jewish Congress' Project for the Study of Middle Eastern Nationalities. He is currently the executive editor of Israel Horizons magazine.

Yosef Gotlieb received his bachelor's and master's degrees from Clark University.